GOVERNANCE OF IT

BCS, THE CHARTERED INSTITUTE FOR IT

BCS, The Chartered Institute for IT champions the global IT profession and the interests of individuals engaged in that profession for the benefit of all. We promote wider social and economic progress through the advancement of information technology science and practice. We bring together industry, academics, practitioners and government to share knowledge, promote new thinking, inform the design of new curricula, shape public policy and inform the public.

Our vision is to be a world-class organisation for IT. Our 70,000 strong membership includes practitioners, businesses, academics and students in the UK and internationally. We deliver a range of professional development tools for practitioners and employees. A leading IT qualification body, we offer a range of widely recognised qualifications.

Further Information
BCS, The Chartered Institute for IT,
First Floor, Block D,
North Star House, North Star Avenue,
Swindon, SN2 1FA, United Kingdom.
T +44 (0) 1793 417 424
F +44 (0) 1793 417 444
www.bcs.org/contact

GOVERNANCE OF IT
AN EXECUTIVE GUIDE TO ISO/IEC 38500

A. L. Holt

© A. L. Holt 2013

The right of A. L. Holt to be identified as author of this Work has been asserted by her in accordance with sections 77 and 78 of the Copyright, Designs and Patents Act 1988.

All rights reserved. Apart from any fair dealing for the purposes of research or private study, or criticism or review, as permitted by the Copyright Designs and Patents Act 1988, no part of this publication may be reproduced, stored or transmitted in any form or by any means, except with the prior permission in writing of the publisher, or in the case of reprographic reproduction, in accordance with the terms of the licences issued by the Copyright Licensing Agency. Enquiries for permission to reproduce material outside those terms should be directed to the publisher.

All trade marks, registered names etc. acknowledged in this publication are the property of their respective owners. BCS and the BCS logo are the registered trade marks of the British Computer Society, charity number 292786 (BCS).

Published by BCS Learning and Development Ltd, a wholly owned subsidiary of BCS, The Chartered Institute for IT, First Floor, Block D, North Star House, North Star Avenue, Swindon, SN2 1FA, UK.
www.bcs.org

PDF ISBN: 978-1-78017-155-5
ePUB ISBN: 978-1-78017-156-2
Kindle ISBN: 978-1-78017-157-9
Paperback ISBN: 978-1-78017-154-8

Ebook available

British Cataloguing in Publication Data.
A CIP catalogue record for this book is available at the British Library.

Disclaimer:
The views expressed in this book are of the author(s) and do not necessarily reflect the views of the Institute or BCS Learning and Development Ltd except where explicitly stated as such. Although every care has been taken by the authors and BCS Learning and Development Ltd in the preparation of the publication, no warranty is given by the authors or BCS Learning and Development Ltd as publisher as to the accuracy or completeness of the information contained within it and neither the authors nor BCS Learning and Development Ltd shall be responsible or liable for any loss or damage whatsoever arising by virtue of such information or any instructions or advice contained within this publication or by any of the aforementioned.

Typeset by Lapiz Digital Services, Chennai, India.
Printed and bound by CPI Group (UK) Ltd, Croydon, CR0 4YY

FSC
www.fsc.org
MIX
Paper from responsible sources
FSC® C013604

CONTENTS

	List of figures and tables	viii
	Author	ix
	Foreword Bill Clifford	x
	Acknowledgements	xi
	Abbreviations	xii
	Tools and useful resources	xiii
	Preface	xvi
PART A – INTRODUCTION TO THE GOVERNANCE OF IT		**1**
1.	**HISTORY OF CORPORATE GOVERNANCE**	**5**
	2000 to current day	10
	Organisational governance	11
2.	**SETTING IT IN THE CONTEXT OF CORPORATE GOVERNANCE**	**13**
3.	**INTRODUCTION TO THE GOVERNANCE OF IT STANDARD ISO/IEC 38500**	**17**
	How did ISO 38500 come about?	18
4.	**THE STANDARD IN DETAIL**	**21**
	Scope and objectives	21
	Framework	22
	Guidance	34
5.	**ONGOING DEVELOPMENT WORK**	**43**
	Guidance documents	43
	Handbooks	47
6.	**BENEFITS OF GOOD IT GOVERNANCE**	**49**
	Cost reduction	49
	Performance improvement	50
	Ability to react quickly to market changes	50
	Bad things that can happen	53
7.	**REVIEW OF PART A**	**57**
	History	57
	The standard – 38500	58
	Benefits	59
	Where to go from here?	60

PART B – IMPLEMENTING IT GOVERNANCE — 63

8. INTRODUCTION TO IMPLEMENTATION — 65

9. BEFORE YOU START ON IMPLEMENTATION — 67
- Benefits realisation — 67
- Need-gap analysis — 68
- Setting expectations — 73
- Using existing documents — 74
- Taking an inventory of existing governance activity — 75
- Test and training strategies — 78
- Recap — 80

10. GETTING THERE – DEVELOPING A PLAN — 82
- Benefits of the modular approach — 83
- Embedding and communicating the plan — 83
- Developing artefacts — 84
- Project prioritisation against the principles — 85
- Reviewing the organisational chart and building your teams — 87
- Reporting on risk — 90

11. ARRIVING AT THE DESTINATION – EXECUTING THE PLAN — 91
- Preparing to roll out the governance framework — 91
- Supporting systems — 93
- Managing project versus operational workload — 93
- Training and testing — 94
- Pushing the button — 96

12. STAYING THERE – MANAGING THE IT GOVERNANCE FRAMEWORK — 99
- Post-implementation review — 100
- Operational management — 102
- Measurement, monitoring and reporting — 106
- Standards, templates, guidelines, checklists — 107

13. MOVING FORWARD – OPTIMISING THE IT GOVERNANCE FRAMEWORK — 109
- Frameworks, standards and methodologies — 109
- Moving forward without moving backward — 111
- Measuring satisfaction – reviewing progress — 113
- Building on success — 115

14. REVIEW OF PART B — 116
- Before you start — 116
- Getting there — 117
- Arriving at the destination — 117
- Staying there — 117
- Moving forward — 117
- Where to from here? — 117

Appendix A: The board report **118**
    Cascading balanced score card example 119
Appendix B: Charter example **121**
    References 123
    Index 126

LIST OF FIGURES AND TABLES

Figure I	Governance-management interface	3
Figure 1.1	Organisational governance at the core of ISO 26000	12
Figure 4.1	Governance framework diagram from ISO/IEC 38502	35
Figure 4.2	Evaluate-direct-monitor activities	41
Figure 10.1	Framework detail example	86
Figure A.1	Cascading balanced score cards in action	120
Table 4.1	Work programme planning	27
Table 5.1	Governance-management value links	46
Table 5.2	Risk management prioritisation	46
Table 9.1	Group questions – collecting requirements	69
Table 10.1	Mapping programme deliverables to the six principles	87
Table 11.1	IT governance framework – assigning ownership	97

AUTHOR

An expert in corporate governance of IT and sustainability management, A. L. Holt is Director and Founder of Longitude 174 Limited and a board member of two charitable trusts. She studied mathematics at Imperial College, London, and went on to spend more than 30 years working internationally in a variety of roles from systems analyst to chief information officer. She joined the world of standards development in 2005, and has enjoyed leading a group that identifies market needs, assesses academic research and delivers timely and relevant international standards.

FOREWORD

Over the last few years, there have been a number of highly visible and very embarrassing IT-related business disasters. The directors ultimately responsible were "looking elsewhere" or lacking the IT knowledge to recognise what was going on around them before it was too late.

Directors don't need to understand the full ins and outs of IT to apply governance over it, but they do need to be able to ask the right questions at the right time to avoid catastrophes. In addition, IT executives, managers, operators and technicians need to know how to articulate their contribution to ensuring that the organisation remains successful and sustainable.

Read this book and learn how to maintain governance over your IT investments and avoid disasters that can threaten your organisation and your own reputation!

Bill Clifford
Ex Managing Director Security Division,
UK Defence Evaluation and Research Agency

ACKNOWLEDGEMENTS

I would like to acknowledge the support of my four children, Lydia, Samuel, Chloë and Esther, in helping me make the time to write this book. I would also like to acknowledge the ongoing ground-breaking work of my standards-setting friends and colleagues in taking our understanding of the subject of the governance of IT further each year.

Ten per cent of the proceeds from the book will go to supporting the work of a trust for encouraging and developing Internet entrepreneurs (the Liz Dengate Thrush Foundation), and most of the rest will go to helping my supportive children pay off their student fees. Please give generously.

ABBREVIATIONS

ASL	Applications Services Library
B2B	business to business
B2C	business to consumer
BiSL	Business Information Services Library
CEO	chief exectutive officer
CFO	chief financial officer
CIO	chief information officer
CMM	capability maturity model
CMMi	Capability Maturity Model Integration
COBIT®	Control OBjectives for Information and related Technology
CRM	client relationship management system
CXO	top executive that has 'chief' in the title
EDM	Evaluate direct monitor
GM	general manager
HR	human resource
ILM	investment logic mapping technique
IP	intellectual property
ISACA	Information Systems Audit and Control Association
ISSP	information systems strategic plan
IT	information technology
ITIL®	Information Technology Infrastructure Library
itSMF	IT Service Management Forum
KPI	key performance indicators
KRI	key risk indicators
PDCA	plan, do, check, act
PIR	post-implementation review

TOOLS AND USEFUL RESOURCES

At the time of writing, there is no neatly bundled IT governance toolkit available that I would recommend. Unlike IT service management where one framework fits all organisations pretty well, the make up of an IT governance framework will depend totally on the culture, goals and characteristics of an organisation. You will be pulling together a mix of standards, frameworks and tools from various sources to meet the specific requirements for your organisation.

Putting together an overarching framework is very much like mixing a cocktail. It requires patience and skill to balance the components, and adding too many components results in a mess that leaves a long hangover. Do not be tempted to adopt every form of recognised 'best practice'. For a framework to be recognised as best practice, it has to have been in use for several years. You might find something that has been developed recently that fits your requirements perfectly, and provides a 'lighter touch' approach.

At the risk of stating the blindingly obvious, a tool is only a tool if it helps you and your business – so do not feel obliged to persevere with a reporting or monitoring scheme that just is not helpful.

Your biggest challenge will be to bridge the governance–management gap. You are aiming to purchase tools that will enable you to monitor and measure governance activity from the management layer, for displaying results at the governance layer, in a way that is meaningful and useful. Once you have read through the book, you will have a very clear idea of what is required and how monitoring and reporting processes can be set up to deliver this information.

TOOLING

Requirements for IT governance tools

There is a requirement for IT governance tools that support a principle-based assessment by enabling measurable outcomes to be linked to principles. These tools cannot be built through empirical means alone, but must be grounded on a platform of academic theory to be reliably useful. Governance runs on a long time frame. If I create a tool to make yoghurt, then it can be proved to work or not work within the space of 24 hours. If I create a tool to assist with the successful implementation of an IT governance framework, the value of the tool might not be evident for years. That said, there are some valuable tools available now that will assist in the building of elements of an IT governance framework, and these are referenced throughout the book.

Interfaces to management tools

No doubt your organisation is already using a number of IT tools, standards and frameworks at the management layer – ITIL®, ISO/IEC 20000, ISO/IEC 27000, COBIT®, CMMi and so on. Your governance tools should enhance the information reported from your management tools, or at least provide a filter for the delivery of relevant, succinct information to the governing body.

There is some excellent material available from government agencies, industry bodies, membership bodies and IT and director institutes in the form of procurement guidelines, frameworks and templates. Your vendors and suppliers will also have research material, white papers, templates and other useful information to guide you with the development of your framework.

CHECKLISTS

Governing body

1. Read Part A of this book and decide on seven key objectives for the development of an IT governance framework for your organisation.
2. Write your own extended versions of the principles of ISO 38500.
3. Ensure that existing organisational policy supports these principles and create new a policy if required.
4. Glance through Part B of this book and read the summary chapter at the end.
5. Encourage your IT executives and managers to read Part B of this book.
6. Work through how you, as the governing body, want to interact with the management team.
7. Provide a briefing paper on what you expect to be achieved through the development of an IT governance framework, and discuss it with your executive team.

CIO

1. Read Part B of this book to see what is entailed in delivering an IT governance framework – policy, process, procedure, systems, services, staff responsibility changes and so on.
2. Glance through Part A of this book and read the summary chapter at the end.
3. Read the briefing paper prepared by your board.
4. Conduct a need-gap analysis to determine how far you are from delivering to the requirements of the governing body.
5. Prepare terms of reference that connect the elements of the framework that you understand that you need to deliver with the requirements of the governing body.
6. Identify potential team members and responsibilities and identify areas where you will need assistance from external resources.
7. Prepare a budget, and the supporting documentation to seek approval and get started!

USEFUL RESOURCES

Committee of Sponsoring Organizations of the Treadway Commission *COSO Internal Control-Integrated Framework* 2011. Available at www.coso.org/ic-integratedframework-summary.htm

Financial Reporting Council *Turnbull Report Internal Control: Guidance for Directors on the Combined Code* 2005. Available at www.frc.org.uk/Our.../Turnbull-guidance-October-2005.aspx

Hoverstadt, Patrick (2008) *The Fractal Organisation: Creating Sustainable Organisations with the Viable System Model*. Chichester, John Wiley and Sons.

Kotter, John P. (1996) *Leading Change*. Boston, Harvard Business Review Press.

Kotter, John P. (2008) *A Sense of Urgency*. Boston, Harvard Business Review Press.

Kotter, John P. (2012) *The Heart of Change: Real-Life Stories of How People Change Their Organisations*. Boston, Harvard Business Review Press.

Baldrige Performance Excellence Program www.nist.gov/baldrige

ISACA Body of Knowledge www.isaca.org and IT Governance Institute www.itgi.org

The Cabinet Office, UK, www.cabinetoffice.gov.uk

Basel II Report – www.bis.org/bcbs/about.htm

Gartner Research – www.gartner.com/technology/home.jsp

TOGAF, The Open Group – www.opengroup.org/togaf/

Lean Six Sigma – www.isixsigma.com/new-lean-six-sigma/

Prince 2 – www.prince-officialsite.com/

PMI & PMBOK – www.pmi.org/PMBOK-Guide-and-Standards.aspx

Sarbanes- Oxley Act 2002 – www.gpo.gov/fdsys/pkg/PLAW-107publ204/pdf/PLAW-107publ204.pdf, www.sec.gov/about/laws.shtml

Companies Acts – for example – www.legislation.gov.uk/ukpga/2006/46/contents

PREFACE

Organisations with good governance practices in place can be shown to be more successful than organisations without.

With the development of IT solutions in all business areas over the last few years, it is likely that there will be very few areas of your business now that are not dependent on IT in some shape or form. If, like other organisations, you have gradually adopted IT solutions over a period of years, then now is a good time to step back and evaluate what you have and what you need to run your organisation. Are you making good procurement decisions? Does your IT supply meet your IT demand?

Rather than look at each business area in isolation, take a holistic view with the idea of developing a decision-making model and a supporting IT governance framework that will guarantee that you meet the needs of your organisation, from the short term to the long term. This is where the ISO standard 38500: Corporate Governance of ICT and this book, which shows you how to implement the standard, can help.

This book is written in two parts for two different audiences – directors and managers, because for an IT governance framework to be successful and to deliver lasting benefits, directors and managers need to work in tandem to implement and to continue to develop the framework.

The first part of the book (Part A) is written mainly for governing board members. It provides a background as to how and why the IT governance guidance in the ISO standard 38500 was developed and how it can be used to direct, evaluate and monitor IT and information management activity in an organisation. It also provides some of the background and history to the governance of IT and the development of standardisation in this area.

The second part of the book (Part B) is written mainly for the CIO/IT senior management team and operational teams tasked with implementing the standard, though governing body members will also benefit from browsing through this half of the book. It provides insight into how to implement 38500 and how to build an IT governance framework, and therefore highlights areas where the governing body can support the deployment programme. It includes artefacts that the author has developed whilst implementing the standard in various diverse organisations. It also includes references to useful tools, templates and other resources that provide a starting point to building an organisational IT governance framework.

Similarly, the CIO/IT senior management team and operational teams will benefit from reading the first half of the book as it assists in developing an understanding as to what the governing body members will be looking for from the deployment of an IT governance framework, and what and how they expect information to be reported back to them to fuel their governance decisions relating to the adoption and use of IT and information across the organisation.

So, are you ready to develop good IT governance practices for your organisation? If so, then keep reading.

PART A
INTRODUCTION TO THE GOVERNANCE OF IT

In essence, the governance of IT is the theory that enables an organisation's principal decision makers to make better decisions around IT and, at the same time, provides guidance for IT managers who are tasked with IT operations and the design, development and implementation of IT solutions.

You could be forgiven for thinking that IT governance is the latest fad or trend to hit IT. However, IT governance has been an issue since Charles Babbage half dozed off on a book of logarithms and came up with the idea for the first programmable computer in 1822:

> I was sitting in the rooms of the Analytical Society, at Cambridge, my head leaning forward on the table in a kind of dreamy mood, with a table of logarithms lying open before me. Another member, coming into the room, and seeing me half asleep, called out, 'Well, Babbage, what are you dreaming about?' To which I replied, 'I am thinking that all these tables' (pointing to the logarithms) 'might be calculated by machinery'.
>
> (Babbage 1864)

This idea resulted in Babbage starting on the design for his Difference Engine – a concept that took almost 170 years to deliver as a product. (Take heart if you are reading this and your IT project has overrun by a mere couple of years.) As Babbage soon discovered, designing it was one thing; actually building it required funding and sponsors. Babbage correctly estimated that a large sum of development money was required. In the 1800s, such an expensive IT project required government funding. This is still the case today.

Babbage had some difficulty communicating his business plan to his sponsors. If we were seeking government money today, we would be unlikely to send the lead developer to speak to the relevant funding agencies. As IT people, we still have issues with describing new or 'leading edge' technology in such a way that non-IT people can understand exactly what it is we are describing. We can also create problems when we send the IT salesman in to speak to the business, especially if they have been trained to never say no to customer requirements and know enough of the fashionable IT vocabulary to sound convincing.

Business has been burnt with keen and ambitious IT companies describing software that has not been written, hardware that has not yet been built. I have heard many a salesman/IT account manager come out of a successful pre-sales meeting having signed a development contract, proclaiming the immortal words, 'Well how hard can it be to build it to their requirements?' Our industry is still fast developing, and we love to use the latest technology to develop our business solutions. Young developers will talk about last year's technology using the same tone of voice that you might use for describing the funeral of a close colleague. We use the term 'legacy system' to describe something that we are too bored to support. No wonder we have problems! But I digress – Babbage had an idea that had huge potential, yet he could not easily demonstrate that potential to his funders. Hindsight is easy. When a Marconi radio was installed in RMS *Titanic*, it was put in for commercial reasons. Nobody foresaw the potential for emergency communications.

> Babbage had every reason to feel aggrieved about his treatment by successive governments. They had failed to understand the immense possibilities of his work, ignored the advice of the most reputable scientists and engineers, procrastinated for eight years before reaching a decision about the difference engine, misunderstood his motives and the sacrifices he had made, and ... failed to protect him from public slander and ridicule.
>
> (Dubbey 1978)

He possibly did not have the patience for sales and marketing:

> On two occasions I have been asked [by members of Parliament], 'Pray, Mr. Babbage, if you put into the machine wrong figures, will the right answers come out?' I am not able rightly to apprehend the kind of confusion of ideas that could provoke such a question.
>
> (Babbage 1864)

In fact he found the whole process very frustrating, and declared to one of his European colleagues:

> You will be able to appreciate the influence of such an Engine on the future progress of science. I live in a country which is incapable of estimating it.
>
> (Babbage 1864)

So ... what is IT governance?

Whenever and wherever a governance standards committee gathers together, it is not long before the question of the definition of governance is raised, or, failing that, the question of the difference between governance and management and where the boundary between the two groups lies. So, why are these such problematic questions to answer? I believe it is because there is such a range of ways that a governing body and a management team can work together.

IT governance is concerned with directing IT-related activity across an organisation – it is about strategic planning for IT in line with the vision and mission of the organisation, and the oversight and monitoring of all IT-related activity. It involves creating a decision-making model for IT and information decisions.

IT management is concerned with the application of IT governance through the implementation of policies, processes, procedures and the management of IT-related projects and other activities. The term IT governance is also being used in some literature for the necessary controls put in place, typically by the IT management team, to ensure that IT governance activities can be reported on correctly. If we refer to this type of IT governance as IT operational governance, then the governing body is less likely to be troubled with operational decisions.

The action of the board or governing body to direct IT activities and to build a decision-making model, combined with the action of the IT management teams to develop supporting systems, processes and procedures, result in the development of an IT governance framework.

Figure I illustrates the relationship between governance (what we do) and management (how we do it).

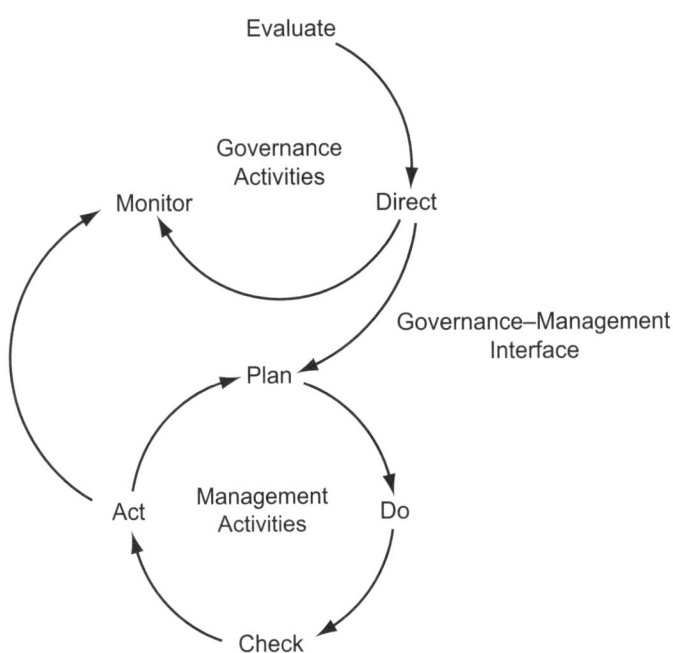

Figure I Governance-management interface

Would IT governance have helped Charles Babbage?

It is always hard to judge the value of something that has not been seen, let alone not even developed. If the representatives from the House of Commons had seen a working prototype of the Difference Engine, I doubt that they would have gauged the potential for such a device. Maybe this sounds a little harsh, but the comment is based on the difficulty experienced by Harrison demonstrating his longitude clock in 1762 to parliamentary representatives. However, let us suppose, though, that Babbage's funders had had an understanding of IT governance. They would have had a sound decision-making model for working through the funding issues. They would have understood the need to resource his project and, in return for funding, they would have set him some reasonable goals so that they could easily monitor his progress.

Is IT governance still an issue today?

Yes, it is! When we published the first international IT service management standard in 2005, there were still many IT teams making live changes to their production environment and now, eight years and a new version of ITIL on, we have seen a huge increase in service management maturity in organisations. By the time you read this book, IT governance issues might be a thing of the past ... but they are certainly abundant as I am writing today. A casual Google search on 'IT project disasters' has just brought back 219 million hits. Partly this is a reflection on how many major projects have an IT element, but it is also shows how the IT element is often overlooked or misunderstood. As we move through this book we will be exploring case study IT governance disasters that range from tragedies through to comedies, and we will pick out the lessons learned so that we can protect your organisation from IT death and IT ridicule.

1 HISTORY OF CORPORATE GOVERNANCE

I believe that, before you can fully appreciate the need for the corporate governance of IT, you need to have an appreciation of corporate governance. There is often confusion around what is meant by corporate governance, and I have heard colleagues talk about organisations where 'no corporate governance is in place'. However, if the organisation is running well, making a profit – or at least not making a loss and meeting compliance requirements in the way of tax and other legal obligations – then it must surely have some form of governance in place?

The purpose of this chapter is to look at the history of corporate governance and to establish that it is not a twentieth-century whim and fancy brought about by questionable financial practices and stock market crashes. Rather, corporate governance is the considered good practice of capable and inspired leaders going back to ancient times. For example, Emperor Tang Taizong created a dynasty of prosperity and productivity that surpassed all others in culture, economy, agriculture and transportation. Taizong ruled from 626 until 649 and his governance was deemed the Confucian ideal – he was a highly intelligent and ethical ruler. He appointed able ministers, kept close relationships with his advisors, took heed to criticisms and led a frugal life. The people who lived under the governance regime of Taizong enjoyed harmony and prosperity whilst the surrounding nations suffered from chaos, division and corruption. He understood the importance of involving his people in governance decisions,

> The emperor depends on the state, but the state depends on its people. When one oppresses the people, so that it only serves the ruler, then it is like one is ripping out someone's flesh in order to fill that person's stomach. His stomach is satisfied, but his body is injured: The ruler may then be richer, but his state is destroyed. Taizong
> (Wu Song 2008)

Too many IT projects thunder ahead without thought for the user who will have to retrain or rethink the way they do their everyday work tasks. Oppression is a strong word to use in this context, but it is certainly possible to upset a stakeholder community through poor IT governance.

His reputation as an erudite political leader stretched well beyond the borders of China. Whilst the surrounding nations suffered from chaos, division and corruption, the people of China enjoyed peace and prosperity.

GOVERNANCE OF IT

Just over a hundred years later, we have the example of Darius I of Persia (c.549 BC–486/485 BC, Emperor of Persia 521 BC–486/485 BC). It is particularly interesting to see the progress made by Darius in his reign, and the order in which he accomplished his achievements:

- First, he sorted out outstanding wars, battles, onslaughts.
- Second, he introduced a system of governance.
- Third, he kicked off some large infrastructure projects.
- Fourth, he initiated and developed economic and trading alliances.
- And finally, he extended the empire overseas.

It is useful to take some tips from Darius's thinking – to make sure there are no outstanding battles across the organisation before you embark on the IT governance work, and to delay the major infrastructure projects until the decision-making framework, policies and processes are established. It is also interesting to ponder on the fact that an organisation with good governance practices in place is in a good position to consider building strong external alliances – and maybe even consider major acquisitions.

Like many CIOs and IT directors, Darius was a surprise appointment – assisted by a team of Persian nobles, he killed the usurper to the throne. The rulers of the eastern provinces saw this as an opportunity to regain some ground, but Darius managed to put down the resulting rebellions. The authority of Darius was thus established. An interesting lesson here is that the rebellious forces within the organisation need to be quelled, and the authority of the CIO/IT director recognised, before effective governance can take place. Darius was a great politician and governor. He revised the Persian administration system and the legal code in an attempt to eliminate bad and corrupt business practices. The lesson here is to tidy up any vendor and internal service level agreements, before embarking on a strategic planning phase. It is unlikely that you will find any corrupt practices, but you might need to address some ambiguities and reset some customer and supplier expectations.

Darius is famous in history, though, not as a law reformer or a great military campaigner, but for his planning and organisational skills. In this he was the true successor to the great Cyrus, and a role model for Herodutus. He limited military campaigns to protecting the national frontiers, and made substantial military reforms to introduce conscription and to ensure his troops were well trained and paid. Internally, he divided the Persian Empire into 20 provinces, each governed by a satrap, who had responsibility for the development of regional laws and administration, and his peers, the financial and military commanders. Together, the three elements made up an executive team that reported directly to the king, who provided ample administrative assistance in the form of scribes – an early civil service. Every region was responsible for paying a gold or silver tribute to the emperor. The system served not only to collect tax to run the empire, but also to lessen the chance of another internal revolt. There are lessons here for the cross-organisational internal IT procurement spending.

Darius took on some ambitious infrastructure programmes during his reign – he built sturdy city walls around his new capital city, Persepolis, he dug a canal from the Nile to the Suez, and he commissioned an extensive and well serviced road network across the nation. The Persian Empire became the envy of it's neighbours. Darius proved that, with the correct authority and processes in place, an organisation can embark on ambitious projects to provide it with a significant market advantage over its competitors.

Darius was also gifted as a great economist and commercial leader, and his reign resulted in a significant increase in population and the development and growth of many flourishing industries. He understood how to build the respect of his people (for example through his no slave policy) and the role of different ethnicities, and he developed the respect of Babylonian, Egyptian and Greek leaders. In the same way, the successful CIO or IT director must understand and deliver to the needs of different parts of the business, and develop some good allies across the organisation. Did Darius make mistakes and errors of judgment? Yes – and it is to be expected in a reign of 36 years! Like all good leaders, he owned up to his mistakes and handled the fall-out from bad decisions with great diplomacy. As IT leaders we will be certain to make mistakes and errors of judgment – it is how we handle them that counts.

It is another 2,000 years before we read about the role of women in governance. In the provinces of Peru, in the time of the Incas (1438–1533), the women learned 'skills related to governance' in addition to Inca lore and the art of womanhood (spinning, weaving and brewing). Inca 'talent scouts' would tour the villages and bring promising young men and women to the Acllahuasis, where they would receive training. Alas, only some of the women would get to use their skills in governance – the rest would end up as secondary wives of the Inca king or rewards to men who had pleased the sovereign in some way. It is an interesting idea – to scour your organisation for men and women who show leadership potential and then to provide them with special training in governance. We spend a good deal of money in our organisations training our staff to manage, but we rarely send anyone other than our new directors on governance courses. Thankfully, we no longer use our skilled women as rewards for our high performing men! Well – not in New Zealand, anyway.

Governance lessons learned from history:

- Establish your authority and develop allies across the organisation.
- Set up clear processes and responsibilities.
- Understand and deliver to the needs of the business.
- Own up to mistakes and handle them effectively.
- Look for leadership potential within your organisation and provide training.
- Tidy up vendor and internal service level agreements; address ambiguities and (re)set expectations.

It is another 300 years before we see legislation around corporate governance and governance structures in the form of the Chartered Companies Act 1837 and the Companies Acts 1862 – 1893 in the United Kingdom. These Acts together cover a range of activities from the governance of seals, stock, associations and registration to the winding up of companies. In 1960, some 70 years later, an agreement was signed that resulted in the set up of the Organisation for Economic Co-operation and Development (OECD) to,

> promote policies designed:
>
> - to achieve the highest sustainable economic growth and employment and a rising standard of living in member countries, while maintaining financial stability, and thus to contribute to the development of the world economy;
> - to contribute to sound economic expansion in member as well as non-member countries in the process of economic development; and
> - to contribute to the expansion of world trade on a multilateral, non-discriminatory basis in accordance with international obligations.
>
> (OECD 2004)

The original member countries of the OECD were: Austria, Belgium, Canada, Denmark, France, Germany, Greece, Iceland, Italy, Luxembourg, the Netherlands, Norway, Portugal, Spain, Sweden, Switzerland, Turkey, the United Kingdom and the United States. Since then, Japan, Finland, Australia, New Zealand, Mexico, the Czech Republic, Hungary, Poland, Korea and the Slovak Republic have joined the original members. The OECD Principles of Corporate Governance were developed in response to a request from an OECD Council Meeting at ministerial level in 1998 to produce a set of corporate governance standards and guidelines. The OECD defines corporate governance as:

> Procedures and processes according to which an organisation is directed and controlled. The corporate governance structure specifies the distribution of rights and responsibilities among the different participants in the organisation – such as the board, managers, shareholders and other stakeholders – and lays down the rules and procedures for decision-making.
>
> (OECD 2004)

The first published guidelines were endorsed by OECD ministers in 1999, and they provide guidance for legislative and regulatory initiatives. The principles were revised again in 2004, and the revised list is as follows:

> - Ensuring the Basis for an Effective Corporate Governance Framework
>   - The corporate governance framework should promote transparent and efficient markets, be consistent with the rule of law and clearly articulate the division of responsibilities among different supervisory, regulatory and enforcement authorities.

- The Rights of Shareholders and Key Ownership Functions
    - The corporate governance framework should protect and facilitate the exercise of shareholders' rights.
- The Equitable Treatment of Shareholders
    - The corporate governance framework should ensure the equitable treatment of all shareholders, including minority and foreign shareholders. All shareholders should have the opportunity to obtain effective redress for violation of their rights.
- The Role of Stakeholders in Corporate Governance
    - The corporate governance framework should recognize the rights of stakeholders established by law or through mutual agreements and encourage active co-operation between corporations and stakeholders in creating wealth, jobs, and the sustainability of financially sound enterprises.
- Disclosure and Transparency
    - The corporate governance framework should ensure that timely and accurate disclosure is made on all material matters regarding the corporation, including the financial situation, performance, ownership, and governance of the company.
- The Responsibilities of the Board
    - The corporate governance framework should ensure the strategic guidance of the company, the effective monitoring of management by the board and the board's accountability to the company and the shareholders.

(OECD 2004)

In 2006, the OECD published an assessment methodology for the principles. This document includes a set of sub-principles with measurable outcomes – a format that could usefully be adopted to create an assessment for the ISO 38500 family of governance standards. In 2008, OECD launched a programme of work to develop guidance documents in response to the problems highlighted by the global financial crisis. This work was published in three phases as follows:

- Corporate Governance Lessons from the Financial Crisis;
- Corporate Governance and the Financial Crisis: Key Findings and Main Messages;
- Conclusions and emerging good practices to enhance implementation of the Principles.

Although the three documents deal specifically with the financial aspect of corporate governance, there are some very interesting findings regarding risk management, evaluation and monitoring. Boards had approved strategy but then did not establish suitable metrics to monitor its implementation. Information about exposures in a number of cases did not reach the board, or the senior levels of management in some cases. Boards found that they could not easily access 'accurate, relevant and timely information'.

> **CADBURY REPORT**
>
> In parallel to the work initiated in the OECD, a succession of company debacles in the UK led to the setting up of a committee in 1991 to investigate the British corporate governance system and to suggest improvements. The aim of the work of the committee was to restore confidence in corporates. This committee was chaired by Sir Adrian Cadbury, and the resulting Cadbury report, entitled *The Financial Aspects of Corporate Governance*, was published in 1992. This report included a code of practice with the suggestion that this code would be referenced by listed companies reporting from mid-1993 onwards. The report includes a very concise definition of corporate governance, and this definition is referenced in the corporate governance of ICT standard, ISO 38500:
>
> 'Corporate governance is the system by which companies are directed and controlled.'
>
> The report makes it clear where responsibility lies:
>
> 'Boards of directors are responsible for the governance of their companies.'

2000 TO CURRENT DAY

There have been a number of IT related corporate fiascos since the 1990s and a number of legislative responses, such as the Sarbanes–Oxley Act 2002 in the US. The current focus of corporate governance guidelines is around addressing risk – and in particular dealing with fraud and corruption, but interest in corporate social responsibility and company ethics is growing. The publication of the corporate governance of ICT standard in 2008 was designed to address some of the residual issues relating to the handling of IT systems and electronically held information. For more information on corporate governance, explore the information provided by the Institutes of Directors across the world. The UK Institute of Directors, for example, provides a range of material including briefings, training, online business support, networking opportunities and access to meeting spaces. Membership benefits include access to subject matter experts on a one-to-one basis. Similarly, the Canadian Institute of Directors provides a wide range of services and materials and access to a news and knowledge database. The Egyptian Institute of Directors provides a number of conferences and seminars for members, training, research and publications. The New Zealand Institute of Directors provides training, guidance and articles relating to the developing area of corporate governance, including a valuable reference book titled *The Four Pillars of Governance Best Practice* (2012). The book is a practical guide to the day-to-day issues of being a director. The basic premise of the guide is that a best-practice board is a value-adding board. The four pillars of value underpin the role of director and board member. They include determining purpose, an effective governance culture, holding to account and effective compliance. Besides providing a wealth of information on governance and building effective boards, the guide also includes a chapter specifically on IT and the board. It could be a useful tool to bridge the board–IT gap.

With the premise in mind that every board is unique and often benefits from independent advice, review and facilitation, the various director institutes around the world work with boards on issues as diverse as reviewing governance policies, practices and board operations, strategy formulation and reviewing governance structures.

The challenge is to find material that resonates well with your board and then to apply the models, practices and policies to the corporate governance of your information and IT systems. If you are lucky enough to have an Institute of Directors close by, you could look at building some customised seminars that help build your IT governance framework into your existing governance framework. The useful supporting services will assist you in appointing directors who will be a good fit to your evolving board.

ORGANISATIONAL GOVERNANCE

I was fortunate enough to be involved in the early stages of the development of the first standard to cover the principles of social responsibility when working with the organisational governance group. We used the term 'organisational governance' to ensure that the standard covered all types of organisation. The 2010 publication, *ISO 26000 – Social Responsibility*, which provides guidance to organisations on various aspects of social responsibility – societal, environmental, legal, cultural, political – lists a set of principles to guide organisational policy in this area (see Figure 1.1). The standard defines the term 'organisational governance' and promotes good governance activity as the hub from which the work to implement the principles can flow. There is recognition that without good governance in place, an organisation, however dedicated to becoming socially responsible, is unlikely to fully achieve goals in this area with consistent quality deliverables. The same is true for IT. Where there is poor organisational governance practice in place, it will be difficult to implement good IT and information practice that delivers consistent quality deliverables. However, where there is good governance practice in place, introducing the IT governance standard should be a simple case of mapping the principles into the existing governance framework. And though the title of the ISO 38500 standard includes the word 'corporate', the principles should apply to any organisation, in the same way that the bulk of the excellent governance material emanating from institutes of directors around the world will bear fruit in any organisation.

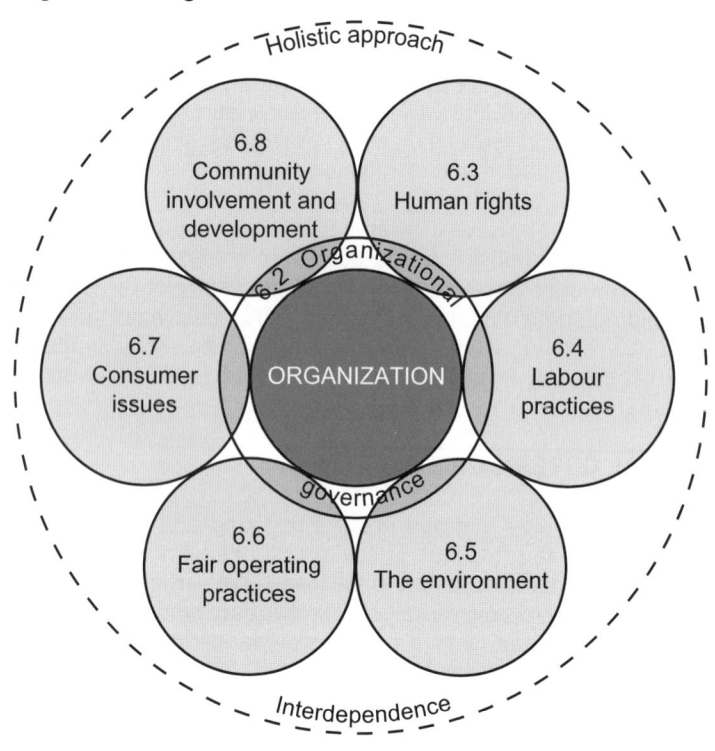

Figure 1.1 Organisational governance at the core of ISO 26000

2 SETTING IT IN THE CONTEXT OF CORPORATE GOVERNANCE

You might be asking why do we need IT governance and not human resource (HR) or finance governance? What is special about IT? What can go wrong? This chapter aims to explain the need for IT governance, and to put IT governance in the context of corporate governance. But first two questions: In your organisation, if the HR director hired 30 people that you did not have jobs for, how soon would that become apparent? If the IT director ordered 30 servers that you did not need, how soon would that become apparent?

Individual directors on a board are used to voting on decisions that are outside their core expertise, but you do not have to be a trained accountant to understand the company's annual report produced by the finance director and you do not need to have a degree in sociology or psychology to understand the psychometric profiling of your staff produced by your HR director. So why is IT an issue? Well, there are two things to note here. First, finance and the HR directors are used to reporting in terminology that is understood. Second, finding good people and looking after the company finances have been two key essentials since companies started back in the 1300s. As recently as the 1970s, IT was the sole domain of the geeks operating a mainframe to provide gnarly statistics – often isolated from the rest of the organisation in every sense. Today, IT is an essential part of the daily life of every member of staff in most organisations. So not only is IT a relatively new area, but it is also still evolving and developing. As with all evolving and developing areas, the IT vocabulary is continuously changing. If you are in any doubt as to this, just try writing down all the words you have ever used to describe computer storage. Now add to this list the different types of technologies used to deliver storage. Also, because IT has developed quickly, we have a number of words that mean different things in a different context. I sit as the head of the New Zealand delegation on the international software and systems engineering standards group of ISO, subcommittee (SC) 7. Recently, SC7 collected together a set of terms used across our standards and, even across our subset of IT standards, we have seven definitions for the words 'change management'.

Maybe directing IT activity will not be such a problem when our Gen Y'ers, who have grown up with PlayStations and X Boxes from babyhood, get to be directors. Until then, though, we have an international standard to assist directors with asking questions of their IT managers, and to provide guidance on monitoring IT activities across the organisation. The standard is also designed to assist IT managers working with their executive and board –to get a heads-up on the level of reporting required and to identify the type of monitoring that needs to be put in place to feed the content of reports that fuel efficient and effective decision making.

So how does setting IT in the context of corporate governance assist managers and directors? It is possible to get a long way up the IT career ladder without needing to be immersed in business practice. A board of directors inexperienced in IT often has to make a difficult choice – is it better to get a technically minded IT director/CIO with little business experience or to get a business-focused IT director who does not fully understand the technical issues? I have seen both approaches fail – but it might be a surprise that, generally, the more-technical IT director is more successful than the business-focused IT director. It is easier to teach a technical CIO the fundamentals of business than it is to teach a business person the fundamentals of technology. I have only seen this approach fail when the technical CIO was a terminal introvert with no ability to hold face-to-face meetings. I have also noticed that a failing technical CIO is often restructured to report into the CFO – especially if the CFO can prove that they have a better idea of the CIO's budget status than the CIO! Help is at hand in the form of the standard. Corporate governance guidelines were put in place originally to restore shareholders' confidence in the running of organisations. In the same way, an understanding of corporate governance guidelines applied to IT can restore the confidence of the directors that their business requirements are understood by IT managers. Following the standard will assist the CIO and IT team in producing meaningful reports, condensing information into useful chunks, and in understanding organisational risk, compliance issues, and the wider stakeholder requirements for IT services and systems.

Boards who are successful in governing IT are not necessarily the ones with members with IT experience on the board. In fact, having a board member who has outdated or a little experience can be a disadvantage. You would not take medical advice from a practitioner with outdated or little experience. IT disasters, like medical disasters, can take a lot of expensive fixing up if they are not handled well, and a serious IT disaster can be life-threatening to the organisation.

Boards that have no IT experience between them fall into two categories. The first type of board delegates all IT governance activities and associated budget allocations to the IT management team to sort out. As soon as IT or information comes up in the course of a meeting, the board flicks the relevant item to the management team without any discussion or thought to preferred outcomes. Depending on the business maturity of the IT management team lead, this practice can range from being similar to giving drinks to alcoholics through to finding safe capable hands to not just keep the lights on, but to strategically plan service delivery to align with the ongoing development path of the organisation. The second type successfully uses a range of subject matter experts to assist and guide the board by auditing and interpreting IT reports and activities, assisting with large IT procurements and reviewing progress on large IT-enabled projects. This can be very successful if the group of subject matter experts is assembled in advance of a major issue or disaster, rather than immediately afterwards. A stitch in time really does prevent nine.

For a board where the IT dialogue is a broken conversation, the standard provides a common vocabulary and a set of pointers as to the subject of the conversation. I have spent the last couple of years working as a virtual CIO for a number of my clients, and I have successfully used the standard to assist boards in asking the right questions and to assist IT management with providing the right answers. The aim of this book is to help you fix up any broken IT dialogues in your organisation, whether you are a board member, a member of the IT team or a member of another business group in an organisation trying to maximise the value of your IT-enabled services.

GOVERNANCE STANDARD IMPLEMENTATION

One of my clients was in a particularly bad way when I started working for them. Across the organisation there were two serious disconnects – the management were unable to have meaningful communications with the IT team, and the board had been badly burnt by a series of unsuccessful IT projects and their communication with the management team regarding IT services was set in the context of risk. Let us start with management and the IT team. The old management had made IT decisions purely based on cost, and with a strategic vision for delivering services that did not extend beyond the current week. If it could be bought for a dollar today and would last a year, or bought for five dollars and last ten years, the one dollar option would be preferred. Also, purchasing was delayed until the very last minute to keep the money in the bank as long as possible. This is not a bad strategy as long as all parties have signed up to it, but it did mean that a request for new back-up tapes would be put through the day the new tapes were needed.

There is nothing wrong with running IT services on the cheap, as long as dollar expense is equated to value, and compromises and dependencies are understood. In IT we need to choose our bargains wisely.

The IT team had got into the habit of choosing the cheapest solution possible, and because every old management–IT team transaction was about buying parts for as little money as possible, all requests were presented as requests for parts. The old management had not really cared why the IT team needed a server – they just cared that the team found the cheapest possible server available and installed it with the minimum of expense. The resulting disparate systems, tied together with home-made code, created an IT environment that was slow and not easily supported or maintained. The money 'saved' was spent many times over on external support.

Along came a new management that instantly balked at the last minute requests for parts described as strings of letters and numbers. They started asking questions, and the answers given made them all the more suspicious and nervous.

Meanwhile, the new board were also feeling suspicious and nervous because they had observed that the old board had paid out large sums of capital for a string of projects that failed to deliver anything useful, and in some cases failed to deliver anything at all. They were keen to understand the state of IT services and delivery and the answers they got back from the new management team did nothing to soothe their nerves.

When I started with the client, I was full of the evangelistic vigour that you would expect from somebody who had just published an international standard on the governance of IT. I had no doubts (and still have no doubts) that introducing governance across the organisation was 'the only thing that could save them now'.

It would have been very easy to deal with the symptoms rather than the root cause, and to become the 'go-to person for all things IT'. I have seen a number of IT consultancies operate in this way, and turn a dysfunctional organisation into a co-dependent, and a short-term contract into a job for life. However, my aim was to work with the organisation and to equip them to manage on their own, with as little external help as possible – to teach them to choose their partner vendors carefully and to know when and how to use them.

So, the client and I started off by developing a short and concise strategic plan to cover the next three years, aligned with the vision and mission and goals of the organisation. We then developed a decision-making model to ensure that all IT decisions thenceforth were made in a consistent manner. We dropped the previous decision-making model of deciding on dollar value only, in favour of making decisions based on quality and business fit first, followed by dollar value. The accountant-minded across the organisation were nervous at first, but soon realised that the organisation was about to stop buying things it did not actually need, and that the new model was not 'money no object', but 'let's find something that matches our needs and then work out which options we can afford'. It took a while for the IT team to adjust to the new way of making decisions, but they soon began to reap the benefits of a procurement system based on business need and common sense.

Three years on and the organisation is transformed. The key IT-related organisational risks have all been addressed through the introduction of tested disaster recovery systems and the replacement of out-of-support hardware and software. Old hardware has been recycled as a full test environment, and the functionality of the home-built legacy software and numerous mini-application Microsoft Excel® spreadsheets have been rolled into a central 'single point of truth' system.

There is still a way to go. As with the introduction of all new systems, the processing side appears to get harder before it gets better whilst the organisation gets to grips with the new features of the new systems and adjusts the appetite for automation of manual processes. However, the client now has a stable platform on which to build and innovate revenue-generating services, and a means to meet the lofty and ambitious goals and vision of its governing body.

Implementing IT governance is not necessarily a quick process, but it is effective. The ISO 38500 standard assumes a blue skies approach, but it is rare that you get to start from scratch with your implementation. Most of the time taken for implementation of a governance framework is spent realigning the organisation to the 38500 principles. However, if you take your organisation along with you on the IT governance journey, you will build up a strong, stable entity.

3 INTRODUCTION TO THE GOVERNANCE OF IT STANDARD ISO/IEC 38500

When the IT department was a small band of computer science specialists sitting around a mainframe computer providing number crunching services to an organisation, it was reasonable to delegate responsibility for IT activity to the key users of the data. However, the role of IT within an organisation has grown extensively and IT is pervasive across all areas of a business, supporting and providing HR, finance, sales and marketing, product and service development and delivery, facilities management, and general information and intellectual property (IP) protection. Directors and senior executives now have a responsibility to ensure the proper use of the organisational IT systems so that key organisational data is available as required, accessible, secure and protected.

The goal of ISO 38500 is to provide guidelines for directors and senior executives on the effective, efficient and acceptable use of information and communication technology within their organisations.

These directors could be members of the board of large corporations, owners of small businesses, or secretaries of public service departments. Regardless of size or sector, unless directors and their senior officers understand their responsibility for governing IT systems, there is potential for a number of problems. I have picked a few examples that I have seen in organisations:

- Different parts of the organisation have different relationships with different IT vendors. This can result in the organisation procuring systems that do not fully integrate with each other. I have witnessed the situation where one part of an organisation was purchasing new PCs unaware of a master agreement that would have reduced the price considerably.
- IT systems evolve across the organisation in an ad hoc way, with no united direction or strategy.
- IT systems over-perform for the requirements of the organisation.
- IT managers have less than a full understanding of the legislative requirements for storing personal data.
- IT users are frustrated by not being able to carry out their work responsibilities efficiently on account of a perceived lack of resources. Sometimes this is just because of poor documentation and users are asking for services that are already available.
- Responsibility for the disaster recovery of a system falls between the cracks where the business owner thought the CIO had plans in place that were under regular review and test, and vice versa.

Unfortunately, some serious problems resulting in issues whose consequences range in severity from financial loss to imprisonment can develop in a way that is invisible to the senior leaders of an organisation. Rigorous disaster recovery is often neglected because of a lack of funds. Living as I do in an earthquake zone, I observe a flurry of activity after each minor shake. However, even here in Wellington, the probability of an earthquake destroying the computer systems of an organisation is less than that of flood or fire. Human error is a significant contributory factor of most disasters that I have witnessed – labourers cutting through Internet cables, somebody powering down an entire server room thinking they were flicking the light switch. The problem is that it is only when some form of disaster strikes that it becomes obvious that the IT department have been operating on a wing and a prayer. Of course, there are ways to ensure that this could not possibly happen in your organisation – and that is what this book is all about.

THE VALUE OF STANDARDS

Standards organisations around the world are, in general, tasked to serve the public good. Suppose I buy a new electric kettle, or jug as we call it here in NZ. I would like to think that I could plug it into a socket – that it would have sufficient pins, presented in an idiot-proof format so as to determine that the right pin fits in the right slot. I would like to know that the kettle is safe to use – I do not want to risk electrocution when I plug it in, and I do not want it to catch fire or melt in use. I also want to know that it meets quality criteria – that it is 'fit for purpose'. I want it to heat up water in a reasonable amount of time (seconds not minutes), and I want the device to have a long life (years not months). In general, standards covering every day things protect us and ensure that we have a quality experience.

IT standards have traditionally had a different focus. They have been concerned with defining and describing consistent processes, common terms, language definitions and so on. The more recently developed security and governance standards, though, are more closely aligned to the standards covering things – they have been developed to provide a safe and quality experience for the users. And thus it is with the IT governance standard ISO 38500 – it is a standard designed to drive safe practices and to create a quality experience for users of organisational IT systems and information.

HOW DID ISO 38500 COME ABOUT?

As a working group convenor of an international standards group, my job was to research international market requirements and to see where my group could add value or provide useful guidance. The ISO process for developing new standards has many endearing qualities, and a number of fail-safe measures that protect us from wasting too much time on something that is not worthwhile. Most of the new ideas and projects that came from my group started off in a study group. To set up a study group in a new area, you need at least five nations to agree that the new area is of interest to them. We agree a scope – and that is generally along the lines of 'let's see if there's any need for standardisation in this area' – and we agree an approach – and that is generally along the lines of 'let's talk to anyone and any organisation that has ever done anything in this area'. We agree a timeline and an output – and that is normally one year to put together a report that can be presented to our formal standards meeting, and circulated round the 35+ nations who are involved in our wider work programme. So, we are expecting a formal report and something of substance, backed up by international research.

New ideas come to us from all nations and all directions. We started work on IT governance in 2006, having discovered a need for guidance in the area whilst running a study group on IT service management. We had plotted a chart of IT standards, frameworks and other guidance against a timeline of how long the average IT process described took to complete, and we made the discovery that there was very little guidance available for IT strategic planning/long-term decision making. So we kicked off a study group to see if there was sufficient international interest to develop a standard. I had our room set up with two sets of white boards and a projector, and I invited all the participants to bring along any relevant articles and presentations. One set of white boards was to catch a set of principles for good IT governance, and the second set of white boards was to collect a set of ideas around what we thought would make a good standard. By the end of the week, we had immersed ourselves in international research, national standards and position papers. We had developed a plan to invite Australia (a nation which ironically had not been represented at the meeting) to present their IT governance standard for 'fast track' (see next section for details), we had started to analyse the gap between the Australian standard and our requirements for an international IT governance standard, and we had started putting together our study group report.

The fast track process

In the 'old days' an international IT standard would have been built from nothing but a vague thought that standardisation was required in a particular area – and some IT standards are still successfully built this way. A draft standard would be created by a group of standards subject matter experts, starting with an idea and a blank sheet of paper. The ensuing rounds of voting, refinement, refinement and voting would take place over approximately five to seven years. Alas, it was too often the case that by the time the final standard was published the original market need had gone away or had been superseded by a new, more pressing need. The idea of the fast track process was to enable a national standard (or similarly validated document) that had been adopted, or had the potential to be adopted by other nations, to be turned into a full international standard by following a shorter form of the refinement and voting process.

Although AS 8015 (the Australian standard for the Corporate Governance of ICT) had not been formally adopted by any other nation at the time of my fast track request, it aligned closely to the guidance provided in Japanese national standards and it was rooted in internationally acknowledged principles of good corporate governance. It also appeared to fit quite neatly with academic research we saw coming from European universities in Luxembourg, Belgium and Spain. The standard was criticised for being very short but I saw this as advantageous – it would act as a basis on which we could deliver a body of knowledge in the area.

I was also very keen that, in introducing an international IT governance standard, we would not displace or replace existing material in the area. In particular, I saw an opportunity to work closely with groups such as ISACA and itSMF to ensure that our standard would work as an umbrella standard over their guidance frameworks and documents. I envisaged our standard being accepted by the board of an organisation who would pass it to their management team to 'make it so'. I expected the management team to then use a combination of ISACA and itSMF frameworks to introduce operational governance processes and controls that would enable easy monitoring and would guarantee the roll-up of reporting from the operational team through the management team to the board, with each level of the organisation seeing the exact breadth and detail to enable them to do their job/carry out their governance role.

It was in this context that we invited Australia to submit AS 8015 for fast track. We were delighted that the standard passed ballot and that, once we had addressed the comments associated with our 'no' votes, we were able to publish the first international IT governance standard in June 2008.

ISO VOTING PROCESS

The ISO ballot resolution process is a fine mechanism for weeding out standards that do not have an international future. Once a standard is deemed to be ready, it is sent around for ballot to the group of nations registered as involved in the development of such standards. Participating nations are invited to express an interest in getting involved with the work and to cast a vote with the understanding that a 'no' vote must be accompanied by comments as to why the no vote has been given. To pass ballot, a standard must exceed the number of yes votes required, must have fewer than the number of no votes stipulated and must have expressions of interest to participate from more than the minimum number of nations.

Once a ballot has been passed, it is the job of the issuing working group to address the no comments through a formal ballot resolution meeting. The aim of the meeting is to discuss the negative comments with authorised representatives from each nation that submitted a no vote and to re-take the ballot to see if some of the no voting nations are then willing to change their vote.

There is much tweaking of definitions and terms to provide a 'one-size-fits-all' solution, but the effort is generally worthwhile. An international IT standard that only worked in a small set of nations would be next to useless, given the ubiquitous nature of IT. Standards need to open up opportunities for international trade, and for that to happen they need to be adopted by as many nations as possible. An example of an internationally adopted standard that many of us benefit from is the ASD-Simplified Technical English standard (ASD- STE100) used by Boeing and other internationally dispersed aerospace and defence companies to ensure that there is a common approach to technical documentation and common naming conventions. It is comforting to think that wherever the 747 lands in the world, there is a commonly understood terminology for the parts used to maintain it.

4   THE STANDARD IN DETAIL

So now we know what the standard does in the way of providing advice and how it came about, let us look at how it is structured. First, we make no apologies for the fact that the standard is short in length. The standard is designed to be read by busy people and is divided into three sections for easy reference, as follows:

1. Scope, application and objectives – covering who should read the standard and why.
2. Framework – covering a set of principles and a model demonstrating IT governance tasks and activities in an organisation.
3. Guidance – providing some examples of how the standard could be applied.

SCOPE AND OBJECTIVES

The scope of the standard is to provide guidance for directors of organisations – those who are responsible for directing activity involving IT resources and who have overall responsibility for ensuring that organisational information and systems are accurate and secure. The term 'IT resource' covers any asset used to deliver information or communication services to the organisation – and these resources could be owned and managed internally, owned internally and managed externally or owned and managed externally. Also note that not all the IT assets will necessarily be under the direct management of the organisational business unit responsible for IT services.

If you bought the standard hoping that all your IT management questions would be answered, you could be disappointed. The aim of the standard is to arm the directors, trustees or those directing activity with a good set of evaluation questions and guidelines for setting up a good decision-making framework for all IT-related decisions. Good decisions can only be made if the decision makers are in receipt of good quality and accurate supporting information, so another key part of the governance activity is setting up monitoring and reporting.

The key objective of the standard is to provide confidence for all stakeholders of an organisation that, if the principles of the standard are understood and followed, they can trust in the corporate governance of the IT provision. If we are to learn anything from the chaos caused by subprime mortgage lending in 2007–2008, it is that governance is not the common sense we all thought it was.

The standard is written as advice for board members, trustees, directors, partners, senior executives or those carrying out governance activities. However, wise IT managers will want to read the standard as a 'heads-up' on the questions that might come to them from above, IT auditors will want to align their services to the conformance aspect of the standard, and IT consultants will want to understand how implementing the standard can benefit an organisation. Internal and external service providers will need to understand the monitoring and reporting aspects of the standard.

The ISO IT governance working group has been working in this area with the aim of issuing guidelines for IT managers working with multiple technology partners. The problem we see is that an IT director, in an organisation running a mix of outsourced and in-house systems, could be dealing with a number of vendor partners and business unit managers, a mixed portfolio of services and products and a resulting jumble of unconnected service level agreements. Everything runs smoothly from the service management side until a problem (or incident of unknown cause) occurs and several systems and vendors are implicated. How are the internal and external providers expected to work together? How do the service level agreements work together? Technology partner governance is just one of several areas that we have been evaluating as a group.

FRAMEWORK

The second section of the standard provides a framework of six principles and a model showing how IT governance and IT management interact, and how all activity needs to span the IT lifecycle from concept through to retirement. This part covers the governance–management glue; the processes that ensure the continual flow of appropriately targeted information between the two domains.

The six principles of IT governance

As a mathematician by training, I would like to know whether all six principles are required to guarantee good IT governance, and I would like to know the weighting that should be applied to each principle. Alas, it is too early to say for certain which of the principles is the most important, and whether all are required. However, we do know from applying the standard that organisations which apply all principles appear to have fewer IT problems than those which do not. From my own implementation of the standard and research, I deduce that the sixth principle appears to be the most valuable. Of all the IT disasters I have had the privilege to investigate, most were caused by human error or by lack of human understanding of the IT system in question.

I have presented on the principles many times in many countries over the last five years. Initially, I used to talk about the positive effects of applying the principles, but I have found that an audience learns more by knowing what could go wrong without the principles in place. So with an emphasis on failure rather than success, we will take a look at each of the principles:

- Principle 1 – Responsibility

    Individuals and groups within the organisation understand and accept their responsibilities in respect of both supply of and demand for IT. Those with responsibility for actions also have the authority to perform those actions.

- Principle 2 – Strategy

  The organisation's business strategy takes into account the current and future capabilities of IT; the strategic plans for IT satisfy the current and ongoing needs of the organisation's business strategy.

- Principle 3 – Acquisition

  IT acquisitions are made for valid reasons, on the basis of appropriate and ongoing analysis, with clear and transparent decision making. There is appropriate balance between benefits, opportunities, costs and risks, in both the short term and the long term.

- Principle 4 – Performance

  IT is fit for purpose in supporting the organisation, providing the services, levels of service and service quality required to meet current and future business requirements.

- Principle 5 – Conformance

  IT complies with all mandatory legislation and regulations. Policies and practices are clearly defined, implemented and enforced.

- Principle 6 – Human Behaviour

  IT policies, practices and decisions demonstrate respect for human behaviour, including the current and evolving needs of all the 'people in the process'.

With an acknowledgement that the principles are not necessarily listed in order of importance, we start with Principle 1 – Responsibility.

Principle 1: Responsibility

> Individuals and groups within the organisation understand and accept their responsibilities in respect of both supply of and demand for IT. Those with responsibility for actions also have the authority to perform those actions.

When we started planning to do some work in the area of IT governance, I was bombarded by suggestions from CIOs from different parts of the world and there was a common theme to their requests, which went something like this:

> I'm a CIO of a medium-sized organisation and over the last two years I have introduced service management processes and policies, tidied up the legacy software, rationalized our vendor offerings (etc. etc.) and we now run a very efficient IT department. However, I have no control over the activities of my peers (CFO, HR manager and other non-CEO CXOs) who continue to purchase software (sold to them as business enablers) that does not fit with the IT environment as laid out in the ISSP (Information Systems Strategic Plan) that has been agreed with our board. I now need to hire additional developers/business support/servers to support the new payroll/HR/product management/ecommerce system, and I will be expected to fund this from my budget.

The CIOs were, in general, advocating a standard addressed to boards to assist with better cross-organisational decision making. There is another point here, though. It is all very well giving CIOs responsibility for organisational IT and IT systems, but if they do not have the authority to say no when necessary, then things are not going to turn out well. I have seen the fall-out from such cases as described above, where the CIO ran over budget and was then demoted to reporting through the CFO. If CIOs do not have a chance to discipline their peers, how much less likely are they to be successful saying no to their superiors?

On the other hand, though, I have witnessed a case where the CIO had all authority and no responsibility and that also turned out badly, with parts of the organisation running on systems and constrained by processes that made their jobs far harder than they should have been. There was a constant war between the IT department and the rest of the business and both sides considered each other to be unreasonable.

The moral of the story is to hire the right people (and remember you cannot add on personality with training, but you can add IT and business skills) and empower your people to do the job assigned to them. It is not just the CIO you need to be concerned about, but the entire IT team. If you inherit an existing IT team, you will have to work with what you have – you probably will not have the luxury of starting from scratch. I advise you to go through the CVs of all your staff very carefully and find out what exactly they were hired for. IT people – especially able ones – tend to drift through an organisation like sheep. One minute they are developing code and the next they are fixing the network on a full-time basis, because they were the only person around when the network went down and at least they understood the instructions for getting it back again. Find out what their skills are and try to put them in a position that best uses them.

Once you have hired the 'right' IT people, or you have shuffled an existing team, you need to write clear job descriptions for them so that they know exactly what their responsibilities are and who they should be engaging with internally and externally on a day-to-day basis. You need to assign them to good managers who will take care of them and stop them from straying across the organisation. For your frontline staff, you might consider sending them on some sort of service management training – ITIL or ISO/IEC 20000. Again, it is easier to hire bright technical staff and teach them telephone skills than vice versa.

> One of my most able and productive support personnel was a young man who was deaf. He answered all 'calls' via messenger applications and he rarely got disturbed when he was rebuilding desktops, so our build quality went up considerably. The local deaf community would send in an interpreter for team and company meetings, and they were kind enough to offer the whole team deaf awareness training.

Once you have your team mobilised ready for action, you need to educate the wider organisation as to what the IT team do and how they do it. You need to set some expectations as to how and when staff might interact with the IT team. I have seen staff hide behind pillars to jump out at passing members of the IT team to ask a question, rather than go through the formal process of logging a support call. I have facilitated a client meeting where we were attempting to find out what was wrong with the client change process. One of the staff complaints was 'we asked for a server and you gave us a server and we did not need a server'. It is a common complaint – a member of staff makes a request, and the IT team member answers the request without asking any probing questions to see if the request is reasonable. Or the staff member makes a request and the request is instantly refused because the request does not fit with the budget/strategic plan/current infrastructure. Neither situation is good. I suggest to my clients that they develop a charter between IT and the main business units to agree on which services will be delivered and how they will be delivered and, most importantly, how new services will be developed and rolled out (see Appendix B). In IT service management language, the charter provides a relationship document that includes an IT service catalogue, an issue management process and a change request procedure. I also coach IT staff to help them ask better questions, or at least to have a discussion around requirements, and to never say no to paying customers.

> Years ago I was an IT manager in an organisation where the HR department decided that their services should be available 24x7x365/6. My team put together a quote for load balanced high availability systems, and it turned out that the HR manager did not have the budget or desire to pay for high availability IT systems. There followed a discussion around business requirements. The HR team were mainly concerned that, if the IT systems were unavailable such that they could not process the payroll, then they would not be compliant to New Zealand employment legislation, and non-compliance came with hefty penalties. To cut a long story short, we came up with a CD based solution that cost less than $100 NZD per year, and satisfied all parties.

Eventually you will find that your IT team will get used to asking better questions and your staff will get used to providing clearer answers. Never saying no to requests involves the requirement to come up with imaginative solutions, and often the most imaginative solutions are also the most cost efficient.

To summarise the first principle, you need to establish clearly understood responsibilities for IT such that all individuals and groups within the organisation, however IT-savvy they are, understand and accept their responsibilities for IT.

Principle 2: Strategy

> The organisation's business strategy takes into account the current and future capabilities of IT; the strategic plans for IT satisfy the current and ongoing needs of the organisation's business strategy.

When we first started researching companies that were good at IT governance, we discovered that they appeared to be more successful than similar companies not applying good principles of IT governance. However, then we noted that the companies that were good at IT governance were good at governance in general. In the same way, I have noted that companies who are not strategic about their use of IT often do not have a clear organisational business strategy. In such cases, there are normally some meaty statements in the organisation's annual report or statement of intent, upon which you can latch a sound IT strategy. And holding interviews with senior managers and board members around the current and ongoing organisational needs can be very revealing. Every viable, healthy organisation has some form of a plan, even if it is short term or existing only in the CEO's head. And most business plans include an IT element, even if it is invisible to the plan's author.

> I have had a situation where I have developed an IT strategic plan to align with the vision and mission of an organisation, only to have the organisation decide to revisit the vision and mission as the IT plan was presented. In the light of my experience, I would suggest that it is worthwhile finding out how widely adopted the vision and mission are before aligning the IT plan. Not everybody will be able to quote the vision, however succinct it is, but everybody should understand the spirit and intent of the organisation.

If you are going to be spending any money, it is probably safe to assume that the organisation is going to be gearing for growth and it is also likely that the organisation will be expecting some form of financial return on investment. Few companies will have the appetite for new IT systems and services whilst they are treading water or are preparing for shut-down mode. You will not always be able to guarantee a dollar return on the initial investment – you might be upgrading systems to meet a conformance or compliance need, or you might be replacing legacy or 'twilighted' software. However, subsequent investment to build systems on your now supported, maintained and compliant platform should be able to deliver services that translate to dollar savings or dollar return.

IT strategic plans can be confusing, so it is not worthwhile attempting to write one plan to meet the needs of all audiences. The board need a high-level plan that gives a rough idea of the required investment and the returns that will be delivered. I suggest that you write the board plan in such a way that the line items, when presented electronically, can be used as hyperlinks to drill down to the detail required for the management team layer, and that the management tasks can be drilled down to provide detail for the operational team.

In Table 4.1 I split the high-level plan into six sections – three vertical sections representing this year, next year and the year after, and two sections horizontally –the things we intend to do (implement) this year and the things we intend to do (prepare) this year, ready to roll out next year. Often when we make an IT strategic plan, we ignore the fact that there are things we need to put in place before we can get started on implementation, and we find ourselves running six months behind before we have even started. The last bottom right-hand segment of the plan should include the planning process for the next three-year plan.

You might be asking whether a three-year plan is too short, but three years is a long time in IT, and the cost effectiveness of different service types is linked to a number of national and global economic factors. Even if your organisation has a very clear long-term plan, it might not be true that the most effective and efficient way to deliver services to, for and from the organisation remains constant across the time period.

Table 4.1 Work programme planning

	Year 1	Year 2	Year 3
Complete this year	Urgent and critical tasks and activities.	Work programme planned last year.	Work programme planned last year.
Prepare for next year	List of activities and tasks to prepare for year 2.	List of activities and tasks to prepare for year 3.	List of tasks and activities associated with reviewing the plan, and preparing for year 4.

In summary, the organisational business strategic plan and the IT strategic plan need to be kept aligned to ensure that the IT provision is always ready to meet developing and evolving business requirements. In keeping the plan concise and succinct, it is easy to modify it to adjust to any change in direction. The process of maintaining alignment is best managed through formal workshop sessions with key business and board representatives. These sessions should be scheduled to run regularly with an understanding that any significant change in the business should prompt an extra meeting. I have found that mature, successful organisations take these sessions very seriously – their key representatives are invited by name and are expected to attend and not to delegate responsibility. Ironically, the organisations that most need to change the delivery of their IT systems to meet their strategic goals are the organisations least likely to see the value in holding a strategic planning session with their IT advisors.

Principle 3: Acquisition

> IT acquisitions are made for valid reasons, on the basis of appropriate and ongoing analysis, with clear and transparent decision making. There is appropriate balance between benefits, opportunities, costs and risks, in both the short term and the long term.

We are very fortunate in New Zealand to have a set of sensible guidelines for procurement freely available from the office of our auditor general. The guidelines are written for public entities, but they cover the full range of procurement stages and predicaments and, if followed closely, appear to lead to good and transparent procurement decisions.

A few years ago we did some international research into the success of IT projects, and we discovered that the failure rate was very high. I am sure that in itself will not be a surprise to you, but there were some surprising facts that emerged.

GOVERNANCE OF IT

There were a number of IT projects that failed to meet business benefits, but there were an astoundingly greater number of IT projects that were kicked off without any thought to business benefits at all. I might just possibly buy the odd pair of shoes without giving consideration to the return on investment or the benefits that I would expect to extract from them, but I would not expect to embark on a multi-million dollar IT implementation without casting my mind to the potential benefits.

Poor IT acquisitions are based on poor decisions, possibly an outdated view of how IT systems work and can add value, or a lack of ability to think with a services rather than parts mindset. Poor IT acquisitions are often made in a hurry – and often by the organisation that did not think it was worthwhile setting aside time to plan IT strategically. Poor IT acquisitions do not take into account alternative options and they are often based on choosing the cheapest solution, even if spending a few dollars more would extend the life of the solution significantly.

Here are a few tips for making good procurement decisions:

- Gain a thorough understanding of required benefits before you start.
- Have a series of informal chats with prospective vendors to help develop your understanding of what you are about to purchase.
- Look for and use good procurement guidelines to ensure a fair, open and successful experience.
- Devise a marking scheme that deters anyone trying to rig the results.
- Visit/find out about organisations that are now doing what you want to do, and see what systems they are using.
- Gain a thorough understanding of the implications of the 'do nothing' option.
- Check out references as early as possible in the process.
- Test your shortlisted systems with your own data and processes through a well written case study before making a decision.
- Do not exasperate your vendors by burning hour upon hour of their pre-sales time with ill-conceived questions.
- Look for systems that can be configured rather than customised to cut down on implementation and ongoing maintenance costs.
- Assess potential vendors to see how well they would work with your staff.
- Review training and roll-out options and make an organisational change management plan as early as possible.
- Make sure you meet the likely project team members before you sign a contract.
- Communicate with the wider organisation through the different procurement stages to ensure that staff know why you are making a purchase and what is expected from it.
- Go and visit vendor reference sites early on.

Time and budget are important, of course, but they are secondary factors in comparison to fit and to requirements, and having the whole organisation understand why the procurement is being made. You are unlikely to be able to modify the time element significantly and, if you do, it will result in a leap in cost and might impact the organisational culture in a negative way. As for the cost, even if the proposed solution is beyond the initial budget, you might be able to justify it through return on investment figures, or you might want to approach the implementation in stages.

Remember that purchasing cloud-based solutions necessitates a modified procurement process. It is possible that by the time the vendor has completed a proof of concept, they have just about delivered your final solution. To manage the risk of purchasing the wrong solution, and to be fair to your vendors, you might consider paying for the proof of concept phase – especially if the work done can be recycled into the final delivered solution if you decide to proceed.

And finally, ensure that IT-related acquisitions are managed well across your organisation. It is unreasonable to expect your CIO to take on support for business systems where they have had no influence on the procurement process. The ad hoc procurement of a business system or package, without reference to the IT team, can result in a security or maintenance nightmare that must be funded from the IT budget. It is also unreasonable for the CIO or architecture team to have the final word on all IT-related procurement decisions, as this can be limiting for the vendor management team who are trying to balance business needs and financial constraints. The answer is to ensure that whoever in your organisation has responsibility for vendor management is mandated to take into account the considered view of the CIO or architecture team when processing an acquisition request, irrespective of the value of the dollar spend. The roll-out of an almost free piece of software can be as disruptive as the roll-out of a replacement fully fledged payroll system if the roll-out results in the need for new support skills or raises new security risks.

In summary, make sure your acquisitions are made for valid reasons, and find out if you can recycle the systems or services they are replacing.

Principle 4: Performance

> IT is fit for purpose in supporting the organisation, providing the services, levels of service and service quality required to meet current and future business requirements.

We can generally recognise when IT systems are underperforming, though it is not always obvious unless your organisation is heavily dependent on IT. We rarely recognise when our IT systems over-perform. It can be very expensive and yet it can come about very easily. We get carried away with a desire for unnecessary high availability, and purchase redundant systems or we replace desktops or laptops with high-end machines that are way beyond the user requirements. A faster processor is a great thing to have for the users doing a lot of processing or heavy number crunching, but the average office user writing emails and producing documents might not notice a great deal of difference. Often we over-procure for reasons of convenience as having everyone on the same desktop platform makes support and maintenance more straightforward. Sometimes we over-procure as a knee jerk reaction to a disaster – we run out of space on a server and as a reaction we run out and buy more space before we have even considered the root cause of our capacity issues.

From an organisational view, the best response for dealing with such problems is to find the root cause for the capacity/performance issue. You might be witnessing a dramatic increase in sales – in which case you would want to procure smartly to increase capacity and performance, and you certainly would not want to disable the service that is bringing in so much extra revenue. Alternatively, you could be under some sort of denial of service attack, whereby increasing capacity and performance will only exaggerate the problem. Even then you probably would not want to shut down the service if that meant losing all sales. You would want to smartly procure a remedy in the form of software or hardware or reconfiguration services to deal directly with the cause of the problem.

As I write this, it is day four of my monthly Internet plan and I have received an email to say that I have burnt through 80 per cent of my monthly allowance of 10 GB. Eek! I am just 2 GB away from dial up speed Internet. A not-unusual IT reaction would be to go out and buy more broadband capacity, but only a few seconds of consideration tells us that this is an expensive problem and that there is probably something fundamentally wrong. First, let us consider the last six months – average use per month is 6 GB and the highest monthly figure is less than 7 GB. My provider suggests that I have evil neighbours hacking into my system. (The call centre representative did not actually use the word 'evil' but the tone of the comment was that used to describe rapists and murderers.) I am concerned that my provider has opted to start charging for Tivo downloads, but I am assured that this is not the case. It is just as well. (For those of you who do not know Tivo, the box monitors the kind of TV programmes that you watch and download, and thoughtfully records 'suggestions' that fit your viewing profile. Our Tivo box is convinced that we are Chinese, and it would gall me to think that I might be paying for a raft of downloads that I cannot even understand.) Obviously, the problem can be 'solved' by turning my wireless router off permanently – and I have seen this sort of drastic approach to solving IT-related problems.

So the moral of the story is that procurement should be made with business requirements in place and an understanding of normal usage, minimum usage and peak usage. For normal operations and depending on the nature of your business, you will want to deliver to the high end or the low end of your normal use. The easiest way to determine how vital high performance is to your organisation is to run a proof of concept on a low performance system.

> I was told the story of a systems manager who was continually purchasing additional disk capacity to meet the needs of the ever-expanding email system. After a while, it became evident that if she continued on this course of action, the system back-ups would not be able to complete in the time allocated. Of course, the answer to this problem was to introduce policy around individual email usage

THE STANDARD IN DETAIL

> and to introduce users to the process of archiving old email, but nobody wanted to inflict policy on the users. Eventually the problem came to a head. The service desk team, gravely concerned that the email system was yet again running out of space, decided to send a request to all the users, asking them to archive their email as a matter of urgency. Surprisingly, it was not the big group email that the service desk team unwittingly used to notify the users that took out the email system, and in fact it was not the email system itself that collapsed. Rather, it was when hundreds of users all attempted to archive their email that lunch time that the file system fell over and apparently took several days and a number of bright systems engineers to return it to working order.

In the case of an emergency where your performance and capacity needs change suddenly and dramatically, you will want to procure a remedy as quickly as possible, but not before ascertaining the root cause of the emergency situation. Even then, you will want to be sure that the 'cure' is not worse than the problem itself.

Principle 5: Conformance

> IT complies with all mandatory legislation and regulations. Policies and practices are clearly defined, implemented and enforced.

Of all the principles, I feel that this should be the most straightforward to work to, but it really is not. Clear requirements laid down in legislation do not always translate into clear direction for IT, and legislation that is hard to get your head around to start with is even more difficult to get your IT systems around. Consulting a lawyer might not be as helpful as it sounds, unless you are really struggling with the interpretation of the law or your method of implementing your interpretation of your requirements involves issuing a warning rather than developing an IT system. One of my clients had a two-stage implementation of policies and practices to meet the requirements of the new copyright infringement laws in New Zealand. Stage 1 did involve a lawyer and a piece of paper, and was relatively straightforward. Stage 2 involved a radical overhaul of the systems providing wireless access to visitors, starting with the purchase, configuration and deployment of a new firewall – no small task.

Another client is getting to grips with the requirements of the New Zealand Public Records Act. The Public Records Act 2005 'sets a framework for recordkeeping in public offices and local authorities'. A key purpose of the act is to 'enable the government to be held accountable by ensuring that full and accurate records of the affairs of central and local government are created and maintained; and providing for the preservation of, and public access to, records of long-term value'. Organisations required to be compliant to the act were given five years to put systems in place. Audits have started and will be carried out every five years. Each audit starts with a self-assessment. The spirit and intent of the act is excellent. With more government data released each year enabling our citizens to self-manage their lives wherever possible, it is essential that the correct versions of the correct documents are made available to the public. Putting in place good record management systems where there has not been anything previously is a lengthy and costly process, but should add to greater work efficiencies over time. From an IT point of view, setting up a record management system is reasonably straightforward. Setting up a compliant records management environment is more complex, but still reasonably straightforward. From a business point of view, though, there are a number of key decisions to be made around what is kept and where, and policy needs to be written to support the desired practice, and to ensure that the practice and policy are maintained. To me, the most difficult element is working out the best option for 'long-term storage'. Neither CDs nor tapes last forever and disk formats evolve and change.

Achieving compliance in IT systems almost invariably involves radical changes to the accompanying business processes. It is essential that business requirements are fully understood, and that somebody in the organisation runs a sanity check against the relevant legislation to ensure that the delivered system will guarantee compliance before delivery commences.

Sometimes becoming compliant is relatively easy and the problem comes in trying to maintain compliance. Imagine that being compliant to legislation means that you need to keep a copy of every business-related email written in your organisation. That is easy enough to do as a one-off activity with everyone in the organisation involved, but the ongoing maintenance to be prepared for an unannounced audit is a headache. As an IT person, your thoughts might immediately go to the ever-increasing requirement for storage and how you can minimise the storage required. As a business person, your thoughts might go to how on earth you will separate business email from personal email.

So the summary here is that compliance can be a headache – for business and IT – but there are three things to remember. First, there will generally be help available from the group who 'own' the legislation, and from fellow organisations who have the same requirement to comply. Second, most compliance activities are viewed as a journey. It is essential to be closer to full compliance this year than you were last year, but it might not be essential to be fully compliant the day the relevant act is passed. And finally, look for a reliable source of information for legislation in development and keep in touch with the progress of legislation that could affect the way you deliver IT services or manage your information. Look for official advice, and help and take it.

Principle 6: Human behaviour

> IT policies, practices and decisions demonstrate respect for human behaviour, including the current and evolving needs of all the 'people in the process'.

Before we jump into the implications of this principle, let us first consider who the people in the process could be, because, as IT has become more utilised across and more engrained in the business, the number of people involved in the process has greatly expanded. In fact, I would be surprised if there was anybody in your organisation who did not have some form of contact with IT. And then there are all the people who read your website, use your web services – competitors, customers, friends, family, colleagues – people from all over the world who connect with you in some way through your IT systems.

Second, let us look at the word respect. This principle is not just about technology – keeping systems running, providing services – it is also about the way you treat your users and ensuring that IT policies and practices support your aim to treat the consumers of your IT systems with the highest esteem.

Imagine that you are a new member of staff in your organisation and that you have only ever really used computers for checking email and browsing the Internet. How good is the induction for using your IT systems? Is it obvious what can be used, and why and when? How good are you at matching systems and people? Does your induction course cover physical set up (desk height, chair, requirement for special keyboards and so on) to prevent operational overuse problems? Do you have ongoing provision for regular eye tests for staff who continually sit in front of screens? What are your policies for using company computers for personal tasks? How good is the training for your corporate systems that are used by everybody – time sheeting, leave application and so on? How well do your internal systems support disabled people? How do you protect the personal details of your staff from access by other members of staff? How do you prevent your IT systems from being used for stalking or bullying?

And what do you count as acceptable use of your IT systems? Are you content for your staff members to check their bank accounts whilst at work? Read the newspapers online? Sit and watch online auctions? Place a bet on a horse? Download music or movies? Read friend updates on Facebook? Tweet the progress of the latest project? Do you allow your staff to connect to your network at work or at home using non-company devices? Microsoft® Windows 8® has a 'Kid's mode', possibly setting an expectation that the children of your employees will want to play with their parents work devices. Are your staff allowed to connect their personal devices to the company network and, if so, how are you controlling the security of your organisational data on their devices?

How your IT policy sets out rules for using your IT systems will depend very much on what business you are in. If reading the local newspaper every day is part of the job, then you will not be blacklisting the local newspaper site. If you are a long way from the nearest bank, allowing your staff to make transactions from their desk will be a bonus for them and might save them from disappearing for long lunch breaks. Do you have a clear user policy for your IT systems? Is there a clear and common understanding of what could happen if somebody was found breaking the policy? Do you have systems in place for collecting evidence for serious policy breaches? If one of your staff members was collecting unsavoury images or illegal copies of DVDs on their hard drive, would you have the forensic skills in-house to deal effectively with the issue?

It is my experience that most organisations only start to consider these types of policy and practice when a serious problem occurs. I have seen examples where the tools used for policing were totally inappropriate and where the organisation's 'police' themselves were the main culprit. Approximately 80 per cent of organisational fraud is committed by staff members within the organisation. If you are going to protect your organisation and the staff who work within it, you are going to have to consider some preventive measures. As mentioned previously, there is ISO work underway in this area to create guidance under the title of digital forensics governance.

Now imagine you are a customer of your organisation wanting to purchase services through your B2B or B2C sites. Are the sites intuitive? Are they easy to navigate? Can they easily be used by disabled people? Is the site colour-blind friendly? Do you make unreasonable demands on your customers? If your customers are forced to register before they can use your services, have you reviewed the quality of the data that you are collecting? Do you measure the number of returning customers versus one-off customers?

And how about the end customers who use your products that have an IT component? What policies and practices do you have in place to protect them and to ensure a quality interaction? Can you guarantee that your deployed software is fit for purpose?

In summary, this principle requires a lot of work across your entire business, involving anybody and everybody who has or will have an interaction with your IT services and systems. It looks like a gigantic piece of work and it is, but look at the huge benefits of having engaged staff using tools that are neither frustrating nor confounding, returning enthusiastic customers and a bank of data that you can rely on to make business decisions and predictions.

GUIDANCE

The third and final section of the standard provides an example for each of the six principles of how the principle could be implemented. This section breaks implementation activity into three categories – evaluate, direct and monitor – which are the three principal activities of the board. This section is not an implementation guide, but it does provide a taster as to how the standard could be implemented.

When we first started work on developing an international version of the Australian national IT governance standard (AS 8015), we were under pressure to replace the evaluate direct monitor (EDM) tasks with the more familiar and widely adopted PDCA (plan, do, check, act) cycle. After much debate, we concluded that it was not only appropriate but also very useful to have a different cycle and to use different terminology for the activities of the board or governing body of an organisation that would set it apart from the PDCA management cycle and the activities of the management team. Mapping the EDM activities to the PDCA cycle, it becomes very obvious how and where board activities interact with management activities, and it highlights the grey areas of confusion where, in practice, individual board and management team members can get very protective and defensive over what they see as 'their turf'.

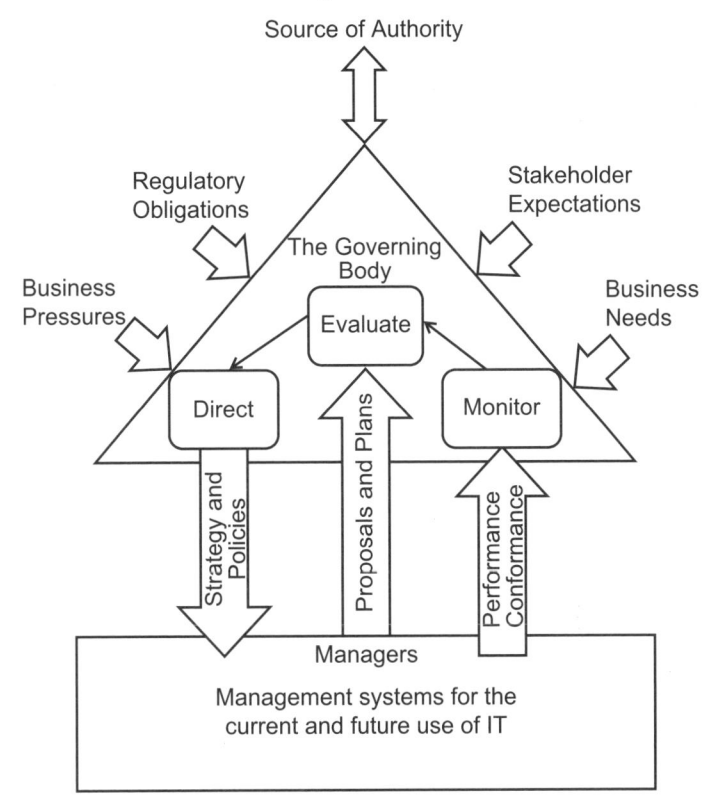

Figure 4.1 Governance framework diagram from ISO/IEC 38502

Evaluate

The standard encourages directors to evaluate continually the current and future use of IT, whilst taking account of the current and future needs of the business. It all sounds very easy in theory, but many boards have been burnt trying to evaluate IT. It can go wrong in two ways – either the information is very difficult to extract or the board are overwhelmed with unnecessary detail and it is a huge mission to work through pages of meaningless reports to work out what is going on. Communication is a two-way street, and for directors to be able to successfully evaluate IT, managers need to be able to successfully provide the relevant and required information (see Appendix A).

The first stage then of 'evaluation' is to work out the desired outcome from a board perspective. The board needs sufficient information to answer the following questions:

- Does the current IT strategic plan align with the mission and vision of the organisation?
- Do the IT supply arrangements meet the requirements of the organisation?

- Are we confident that our procurement strategy and ongoing activities meet our requirements to balance benefits, opportunities, costs and risks for the short term through to the long term?
- Are we confident that we have the right people in the right roles managing our IT and information assets?
- Are our IT systems and services compliant and enabling our staff to be compliant with legislation, regulation and our internal policies?
- Do our IT policies, practices and decisions continue to demonstrate respect for all the people who have interaction with our IT systems and services – internally and externally?

And finally the catch-all question:

- What are the key IT-related organisational risks that we should be concerned with?

If you are a board member reading this, you might be asking why you cannot delegate responsibility for answering these questions to your CIO. As a board member writing this, I can assure you that you will be privy to information that the CIO will not have visibility of. For example, you have a clear idea of the key economic, political and social trends and influences that are affecting and will affect the business in the next few years. You will also have a clear idea of where the business is heading in the next one, three and five-year time periods. You need to know that you can maintain competitive advantage, protect developing and developed IP and sustain your market differentiators, and all of these have IT components or associated IT activities. Your organisation might be planning partnerships, mergers or acquisitions, or just planning to share back office services with another organisation – and any of these would have implications for IT delivery and IT service provision. And, finally, you will be privy to financial information – actual and forecast figures – that will influence your view on procurement and supply.

If you are a manager or CIO reading this, you might be perplexed as to what you should be providing to your board in the way of information and reports to enable them to make accurate evaluations. You do not want to provide too little or too much information and you want to provide it in an easily readable format without dumbing it down. Also, you probably see what happens today and what could happen tomorrow as two very different scenarios, so you will want to present the current situation with a 'heads-up' on the future. From the paragraph above, you can see that you might not have a clear and accurate view of the long-term future of the organisation, so you can only report against the published plans, but that will be sufficient for the board.

Before any reports change hands, develop a template that covers all the bases for the information required and sets an expectation for the level of detail required. Test out different formats and presentation methods. The board of one of my clients does absolutely everything in Microsoft PowerPoint® and it works very well for them. Dashboards with the ability to drill down into increasingly more detailed information have been very popular.

THE STANDARD IN DETAIL

> Speaking as a board member, I am a big fan of the cascading balanced score-card approach (see Appendix A), where different score cards are set up for each level of the organisation, but each lower layer feeds into the level above and the score cards can be read from the bottom up or from the top down. This approach is great for diagnosis when things do not go to forecast. The board wants to know that everything is fine and dandy, without having to wade through pages of reports. However, if there is something that gives cause for concern, they are going to want to dig deeper to see what is happening. The beauty of the cascading score-card approach is that information collected from the operational team can be summarised as part of the management reporting information, and this can then be summarised for the board. Now, if a member of the board wants to reverse the process, they can dig down to the raw data that informed the high-level report that they are looking at.

One of the faults with current governance and management practice is that it is fuelled by the notion that the higher up you are in an organisation, the less you need to know about operational detail. And yet, when we look at some of the recent security failures of European organisations, the source of the errors has been at the coal-face in the operational detail.

One of my colleagues likens the art of governance to steering a ship. I do not need to know absolutely everything about the ship to steer it, but there are some useful indicators that will help me make my decision as to where to steer it. As a board member, I am looking for patterns and anomalies. In the case of the ship, I check that I have enough fuel to reach my destination. If on day two of my voyage, I have used considerably more fuel than I would have expected, I am going to want to know more information than the dashboard view of the fuel gauge can provide. I am going to want to know whether I have a leaky fuel tank or a faulty gauge, and I am going to want to know the information pretty quickly.

Cascading balanced score cards give the board the tools to dig into information as and when they want, without waiting for the next board meeting.

Let us suppose that the cost of producing one of the products has gone up this month and there has been some arm-waving about increasing fuel prices. If the board member is only two clicks away from operational costs on an online report, he/she can find out instantly what is actually going on, without calling a meeting or waiting for management to hold an enquiry.

If you constantly tune your cascading score cards, you will refine the information collection and restrict the indicators to ones that provide reliable and useful knowledge.

My 'perfect board report' is less than one page long, and shows a high-level summary position of everything I am interested in (see Appendix A). It provides a status report addressing all six of the governance principles, shows an ISO 31000 compliant pie chart distribution of risk before and after planned mitigation with one sentence on each of the highest risks, a budget summary and, lastly, presents recommendations for board sign-off.

Providing reports to enable the board to evaluate how the organisation is faring against the six principles will depend largely on the size and nature of the organisation. There is an interesting jurisdictional aspect to consider when addressing the evaluation of your conformance requirements and the human behaviour elements. Conformance should be straightforward and easily trackable, but the human behaviour elements need considerable thought if your services are available globally. What might be considered respectable for users in your country might be an insult to users in other parts of the world.

With all new reporting schemas, the best approach is always to start large and modify or cut away the bits that prove not to be useful or informative. By all means operate a regular reporting schedule, but set an expectation that you will want to receive additional reports when particular circumstances arise or specific events trigger an urgent need for information. If you can give your IT team the 'heads-up' on the sorts of reports you might want to see as a result of particular events, they can set up triggers in advance. As a board it is worth listing the types of events (including unexpected successes as well as disasters) that would trigger the need for urgent reports, and passing on the list to the IT management team before such an event occurs. The purpose of evaluating your IT systems and services is to ensure that the organisation is fit to handle all and any challenges, good and bad, that come its way.

Direct

The standard describes boards directing the preparation and implementation of plans and policies.

> Directors should assign responsibility for, and direct preparation and implementation of plans and policies. Plans should set the direction for investments in IT projects and IT operations. Policies should establish sound behaviour in the use of IT.
> (ISO/IEC 38500 2008)

This is directing in the spirit of Star Trek – 'make it so'. It is not about getting involved in the writing of plans and policies, but neither is it about delegating authority for determining appropriate plans and policies to your IT management team. If you are unable to determine what a suitable set of plans and policies might look like for your organisation, get assistance in the form of a facilitated session for your board from a respected IT/business guru. By the time you realise that your plans and policies are lacking in some way, it might be too late for you or your organisation. Also, do not just try and copy over the plans and policies from another organisation. Even if they run a similar business, they are unlikely to have a similar organisational culture. And if perchance they do tick both of those boxes and you copy their plans and policies, where is your competitive advantage?

First, before you can consider directing activities here, you need to know what the outcome should be. You would be ill-advised to order your management team to 'make it so' if you do not know what having 'it so' looks like. You do not arrive at a train station and idly jump on the first train that comes along because you need to catch a train. And so it is with plans and policies – you will get on better if you understand the destination and have an idea of how quickly you want to arrive there before you can embark on the journey.

Second, boards are encouraged in the standard to direct and oversee the transition of projects from development into production.

> Directors should ensure that the transition of projects to operational status is properly planned and managed, taking into account impacts on business and operational practices as well as existing IT systems and infrastructure.
> (ISO/IEC 38500 2008)

This might on the face of it sound like an operational task for a board to perform. However, I know many organisations that have lost money through poor transition of IT systems or the introduction of new IT-enabled systems and services. It is perfectly reasonable to delegate the physical switchover of systems or services to an accomplished IT team, but the IT team cannot be expected to be aware of, or responsible for, the full organisational impact of the change. It is far, far easier to direct and own this activity from the outset and before the change than to clear up any fall-out after the transition has completed. If the operational risk of having systems and services unavailable is not sufficient motivation, there's the financial risk of losing money from services that cannot be delivered fully or invoiced, and the reputational risk of being seen to run unreliable or faulty systems and services.

Third, boards are advised to direct or encourage the development of a good governance culture within their organisation.

> Directors should encourage a culture of good governance of IT in their organisation by requiring managers to provide timely information, to comply with direction and to conform with the six principles of good governance.
> (ISO/IEC 38500 2008)

I have observed organisations where the board members are consistently late to meetings and, when they arrive, they check their phones and start responding to emails. They are continually running behind, and they are never fully present anywhere, because they are trying to catch up on the outcomes of the last meeting they attended. The senior managers in the organisation exhibit the same behaviour and so it flows on down the organisation. I use this as an example, not of bad behaviour, but of how the behaviour of the leaders of an organisation will be modelled by the next level down and so on, until the behaviour is adopted throughout the organisation and becomes part of the organisational culture. If, as board members, you are going to develop and direct a culture of good governance, you must first model it. The old adage, 'don't do as I do, do as I say' just does not work when it comes to developing good basic organisational behavioural patterns.

GOVERNANCE OF IT

Yet, just modelling good governance alone will not guarantee adoption. You will need to set some very clear expectations for your managers around reporting, completing what they have been tasked to do in the way that they have been tasked to do it, and in adhering to the six principles of the standard. Depending on your organisational culture, you might want to utilise some visual aids or 'aides memoire' in the form of calendar reminders, posters and so on, or you might want to assign and reward the organisational champions who embrace good governance principles.

And, finally, the standard exalts boards to intervene, if necessary, where situations require an escalated response.

> If necessary, directors should direct the submission of proposals for approval to address identified needs.
> (ISO/IEC 38500 2008)

As a board member you might observe a cross-organisational issue or an urgent issue that might not fit within the responsibility of any one particular senior manager. Do not confuse 'directing the submission of proposals' with 'submitting proposals'; and take special care not to confuse 'if necessary' with 'as a general rule', and all will be well.

Monitor

The third board member activity promoted by the standard is 'monitoring'. Interestingly, I have met many boards who carry out two of the three activities, but not many who carry out all three. The activity that gets dropped tends to be either evaluating or monitoring. Boards that evaluate and direct but do not monitor set an expectation that performance does not matter and outcomes are not important. Boards that direct and monitor but do not evaluate can set staff on edge or put them in a permanent state of confusion – they are possibly being marked on something where they have no idea what they are expected to do.

The diagram on Figure 4.2 shows how the governance activities of evaluate, direct and monitor work together.

If you think of the evaluate-direct-monitor model as three parts of a cycle rather than as three independent activities, it becomes clear that, having evaluated what needs to be done, the board can direct activities to meet requirements and to deliver in the short and long term. Then, having set everything in place, the board can monitor outputs and outcomes to check that the organisation meets internal and external obligations for performance and compliance, that all associated and related activities are in line with the stated strategy and that they demonstrate respect for all the people involved along the way.

> Directors should monitor, through appropriate measurement systems, the performance of IT. They should reassure themselves that performance is in accordance with plans, particularly with regard to business objectives. Directors should also make sure that IT conforms with external obligations (regulatory, legislation, common law, contractual) and internal work practices.

> Note: Responsibility for specific aspects of IT may be delegated to managers within the organisation. However, accountability for the effective, efficient and acceptable use and delivery of IT by an organisation remains with the directors and cannot be delegated.
>
> (ISO/IEC 38500 2008)

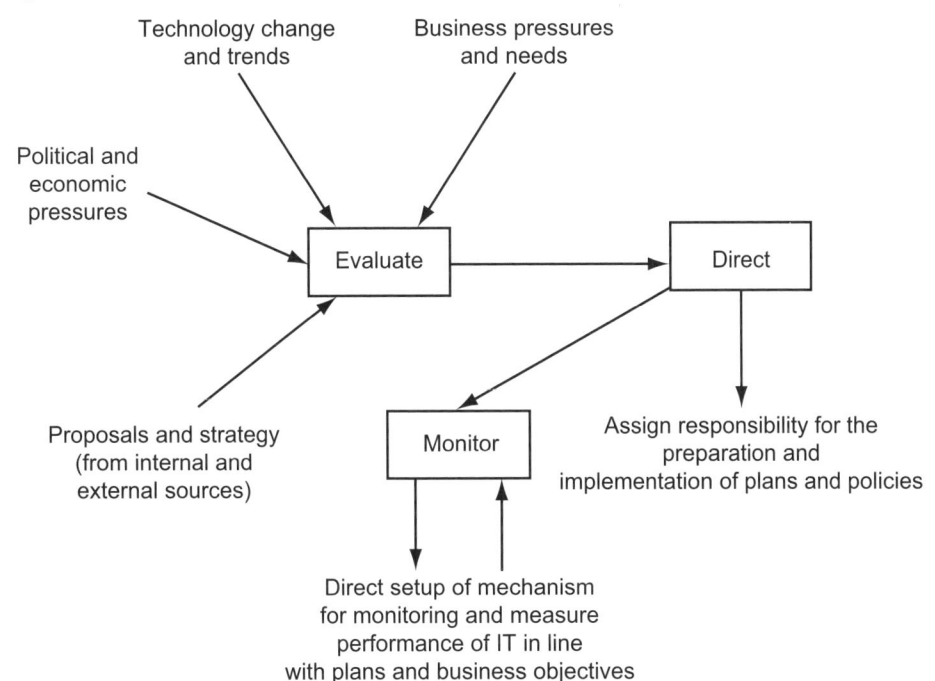

Figure 4.2 Evaluate-direct-monitor activities

```
     Technology change    Business pressures
       and trends           and needs
                \              /
Political and    \            /
economic          \          /
pressures  ─────→ ┌──────────┐ ──────────→ ┌────────┐
                  │ Evaluate │              │ Direct │
                  └──────────┘              └────────┘
                 ↗      │                        │
                /       ↓                        ↓
Proposals and strategy  ┌─────────┐    Assign responsibility for the
(from internal and      │ Monitor │         preparation and
external sources)       └─────────┘    implementation of plans and policies
                            ↕
              Direct setup of mechanism
              for monitoring and measure
               performance of IT in line
             with plans and business objectives
```

It is obvious that the board must be responsible for the legal compliance aspects of IT provision and delivery, and board members should be aware that non-compliance could result in a jail sentence. The standard also makes it very clear that monitoring the effective, efficient and acceptable use and delivery of IT by an organisation cannot be delegated. Ineffective, inefficient IT systems can cause organisations to go out of business. Unacceptable use and poor delivery of IT can result in reputation loss that sticks forever.

For the senior IT managers, 'being monitored' by the board should be seen as an opportunity to demonstrate wise investment and not be seen as a threat to delivery or innovation. Once the EDM activities are well understood and working efficiently, there should be a clear communication path between the board and the IT senior managers, ensuring that money spent on IT systems and services is invested with discernment and prudence, delivers expected benefits and maintains a compliant and user-friendly working environment.

Guidance through evaluate-direct-monitor activities

The standard usefully concludes with a section demonstrating how the lifecycle activities can be applied to each principle. The activities provide the basis for practice documents aligned with each of the six principles, though they are far from exhaustive. Given that these practices will need to be made organisation-specific, the aim is to provide some working samples that can be expanded upon.

5 ONGOING DEVELOPMENT WORK

The framework for the control of IT that combines the six principles (responsibility, strategy, acquisition, performance, conformance, human behaviour) and the three tasks (EDM), together with the generic examples of aligning the tasks with the principles, make up the core of the Corporate Governance of ICT standard ISO/IEC 38500, which serves as general guidance to directors.

The framework within the standard will be the basis for more detailed guideline documents in the form of international standards, technical reports and handbooks. We are developing a series of IT governance framework standards by applying the six principles and the EDM activities to evolving areas where we feel standardisation would add value.

The standard, ISO/IEC 38500, though addressed to the board of an organisation as the primary audience, has been applied more widely to assist senior business managers of organisations in their governance of new initiatives (projects) and of operations. The Australian (and original) version of the standard (AS 8015) was part of a family of Australian corporate governance standards. The UK is also taking a leading role in the area of developing governance standards. Standard BS 13500 is a code of practice for delivering effective governance. Like the Japanese corporate governance standards, these standards work well alongside the IT governance standards. Corporate governance areas covered by these various national standards include:

- fraud and corruption control;
- organisational codes of conduct;
- corporate social responsibility;
- whistle blower protection programs for entities;
- projects involving an information technology investment;
- records management and knowledge management.

National standards have the advantage of aligning with national legislation.

GUIDANCE DOCUMENTS

Within a year of the publication of 38500, the IT governance work was split across two groups in ISO. One group took responsibility for maintaining the published standard and developing supporting documents to assist with the implementation. The second group, which I chaired, took responsibility for applying the 38500 standards to different areas of IT and developing IT governance frameworks. Before the two work programmes merged back together at the start of 2013, my group was creating IT governance framework guidance in the following areas:

Cloud computing – We developed a technical report providing advice for organisations looking to procure services hosted in the cloud. I used the report with one of my clients last year. It took the mystery and confusion out of cloud procurement, and helped them focus on the service delivery elements that were important to them, and to obtain assurance for the areas that they considered to be of the highest risk.

IT audit – We were developing a technical report providing guidance as to how audit should be carried out in an organisation, using the principles of ISO/IEC 38500 and adding sub-principles with measurable outcomes. The final document will be created with reference to the OECD guidelines on principle-based assessment. The foreword to the standard presents the objectives as follows:

> As IT is increasingly becoming more diversified and complex and becoming ever more coupled with front office activity in the delivery of systems and services, IT related risks are becoming more prominent and realizing value from IT is becoming increasingly difficult. The importance of good governance of IT and ensuring that IT is seen as a corporate tool as opposed to a corporate cost is increasingly becoming a crucial and complex issue for organisations to realise.
>
> Under these circumstances, IT Audit is seen as an effective means to ensure IT risks are properly managed and the value of IT can therefore be appropriately delivered in a controlled and well executed way. IT Audit plays a prominent role and an important object in the overall governance of IT. The objective of this guideline is to provide guidance on IT Audit which assures efficient, effective and acceptable use of IT based on the principles as specified in ISO/IEC 38500.
>
> (Extract from the scope of WD ISO/IEC 30120 IT Audit – Audit guidelines for Governance of IT)

Digital forensics – In conjunction with the IT security management group in ISO, we produced a draft international standard providing guidance on the prudent strategic preparation for the digital investigation of an organisation. The following is an extract from the scope of the standard. We envisage the final standard being used by company boards to ensure that they are prepared for difficult situations (fraud, theft, and other forms of illegal use of IT and information systems) before they occur.

> Organisations of any kind face both internal and external factors and influences that can lead to the occurrence of legal actions and placement of demands on the Information Technology (IT) and related Information Systems (IS) to disclose digital evidence. The occurrence of legal action may be the result of an uncertain, unplanned or unexpected event or it may occur as a planned course of action

against employees, competitors or service suppliers. Whether a risk is significant or not will depend on the level of risk and the organisation's risk attitude. Its risk attitude will be reflected in its risk criteria. Because it is almost certain that digital evidence will be discovered and therefore subject to legal disclosure, organisations should plan and develop capability to deal with such legal actions before they occur.

This International Standard is about the prudent strategic preparation for digital investigation of an organisation. Forensic readiness assures that an organisation has made the appropriate and relevant preparation for treating potential events of an evidential nature. Actions may occur as the result of inevitable security breaches, fraud, and reputation assertion. In every situation IT should be strategically deployed to maximise the effectiveness of evidential availability, accessibility and cost efficiency. The responsibility of the Governing body is to provide strategic direction in all matters of relevance to the organisation. The Governing body is informed by principles of best practice that provide general guidance on matters of certainty and compliance. These principles may come from legal mandates, standards, or social and cultural imperatives. In this International Standard the principles come from the ISO/IEC 38500:2008 for the guidance of best practice of IT governance (Clause 4).

Principles require implementation. The actions of governance are to Monitor, Evaluate and Direct strategic policy execution. The stakeholders of an organisation provide the mandate for governance and the Governing body has the ultimate ownership of risk. A framework for the governance of digital forensic risk is established by the owners of risk taking appropriate actions to assure the strategic direction of the organisation. Hence the goal of governance is to provide continuous articulation of strategic direction through the framework (Clause 5). The framework requires strategic processes to deliver direction to executives and top managers. The strategies for treating Digital Forensic risk are principally archival, discovery, disclosure, capability, and profile compliance (Clause 6). The Goals derived from the Principles are measureable through Goal Performance Indicators (KGIs), the strategic objectives derived from the strategies are measurable through the key performance indicators (KPIs), and the variation between the KGIs and the KPIs measures is an indication of the business performance (KBIs) (Clause 7).

This standard should be used in conjunction with the guidance contained in ISO 31000 Risk management – Principles and Guidelines; and ISO/IEC 38500 Corporate Governance of Information technology.

(Extract from the scope of CD ISO/IEC 30121 Governance of Digital Forensic Risk Framework)

Interoperability – our ad hoc group looking at interoperability was almost overwhelmed by the number of issues perceived in the marketplace relating to this subject. We spent our first year trying to define the interoperability issues relating to social networking, the use of consumer devices in a business domain, data exchange and business alignment. We came up with the information given in Table 5.1, which we considered using as the starting point for a second piece of work. If we continue the work, our aim would be to build a framework of principles and sub-principles that address the issues of interoperability in different domains, and link to outcomes that can be measured at the management level.

Table 5.1, taken from an SC7 Study Group Report on the 'Governance of Consumer IT in a Business Domain', identifies the value links that take the governance principles through to management activities, and maps these value links to the interoperability issues identified.

Table 5.1 Governance-management value links

Governance principles	Value link	Management proxies
Responsibility	Reliability	Accountability
Strategy	Measurability	Objectives
Acquisition	Consistency	Procurement
Conformance	Alignment	Controls
Performance	KBIs	KPIs
Human Factors	Flexibility	Contracts

Table 5.2 (taken from the same SC7 Report on the 'Governance of Consumer IT in a Business Domain') demonstrates how a risk management priority matrix can highlight priority areas for applying resource and effort.

Table 5.2 Risk management prioritisation

| Value link | Economic opportunity | | | |
	Social networking	Business alignment	Commodity services	Data exchange
Reliability	Medium	High	High	High
Measurability	Medium	High	High	Medium
Consistency	Medium	Medium	High	High
Alignment	High	Medium	Medium	High
KBIs	Medium	Low	High	High
Flexibility	Medium	Low	Medium	High

Business frameworks – The Business Frameworks Study Group worked on mapping the Business Information Services Library (BiSL) framework to the principles of ISO/IEC 38500. The BiSL, previously known as the Business Information Service Management Library, is a framework used for information management. BiSL has been a public domain standard since 2005, governed by the ASL BiSL foundation (previously ASL Foundation). The framework describes a standard for processes within business information management at the strategy, management and operations level. BiSL is closely related to the ITIL and ASL framework, yet the main difference between these frameworks is that ITIL and ASL focus on the supply side of information (the purpose of an IT organisation), whereas BiSL focuses on the demand side (arising from the end-user organisation).

Once the BiSL mapping work is complete, other frameworks will be considered for mapping to the 38500 principles. The early mapping work we did with ISO/IEC 20000 to ITIL and other service management frameworks proved invaluable for organisations wanting to take an easy adoption path to the standard.

Finally, in May 2012, we kicked off a new piece of work in the area of human usability and the ethical use of IT. After years of discovering that most IT failures have a strong human element/cause, it is a research area that I am particularly excited about. And we will most likely touch on some ethical principles concerning governance of the Internet. The combined ISO governance group will be taking on the support and maintenance of the 38500 standard, together with the development of associated IT governance frameworks, and will continue to provide useful guidance for those embarking on an IT governance journey.

HANDBOOKS

We get a lot of feedback through ISO channels that the standards in themselves might provide good guidance, but most users will require some sort of handbook or implementation guide to make the most of the advice provided. A number of handbooks are also planned or in development to assist with creating the detailed procedures necessary for implementing the standards.

These include organisation type specific handbooks:

Procedures for Corporate Governance of ICT in Corporations
Procedures for Corporate Governance of ICT in the Public Sector
Procedures for Corporate Governance of ICT in Small to Medium Enterprises

Handbooks covering specific topics:

Build and Use of Business Cases
Preparation of Strategic Plans
Plan, Produce, and Use Information Policies

Handbooks to assist with the setting up of appropriate evaluate, monitor and direct activities:

Evaluate and Monitor Procurement of ICT
Monitor the ICT Support of the Organisation

And, finally, handbooks aimed particularly at industries and sectors where governance is key. These handbooks will work well in conjunction with the *Introduction to Corporate Governance* and *Applications of Corporate Governance* handbooks published by Standards Australia.

The IT governance work continues.

6 BENEFITS OF GOOD IT GOVERNANCE

Organisations working from the 38500 six principles of best practice IT governance, and using a tried and tested decision-making model to evaluate business cases and to guide procurement decisions, can expect to see the following benefits:

- cost reduction;
- performance improvement;
- ability to react quickly to market changes;
- increased customer satisfaction;
- more sustainable practices;
- increased revenue per dollar cost;
- general workplace benefits for the board, management and staff.

COST REDUCTION

Cost reduction does not happen overnight. Introducing IT governance has a cost attached. However, over the course of 18 months to two years, you would expect to be able to deliver IT-enabled services at lower cost. Several factors contribute to the lower cost. Having a clearly defined strategy that is aligned with the organisation's goals and mission will enable the culling of services and systems that are no longer required. Matching capacity delivered to what is required will reduce waste – either of spare IT capacity or staff sitting around waiting for computer resources to respond.

> Cost analysis of desktops and desktop support at the local university a few years ago resulted in new leased PCs being supplied to all staff and students. Previously, university staff would receive new desktops and they would pass on their old machines to their PhD students. IT desktop support staff were spending the majority of their time maintaining and repairing the old machines for the students. Replacing every desktop throughout the university freed up desktop support time for rolling out applications and supporting the teaching staff.

PERFORMANCE IMPROVEMENT

Performance improvement comes from matching performance required to performance delivered. Overdelivery of performance can be invisible and is often the result of a misunderstanding between business owners and the IT team or the work of an overenthusiastic IT team. I have witnessed highly specified, high performing IT equipment linked together with a bottleneck of a slow network. I have heard businesses demand high availability systems, when really they only wanted high availability from 9 a.m. to 5 p.m., Monday to Friday. I have seen executives issued with computers with the processing power to run the analysis for a cancer research laboratory, when really all they want is a tablet computer or large smartphone for collecting email.

Underdelivery of IT systems can also be invisible. Staff get used to slow systems and working around the inconvenience – making cups of coffee whilst their PC boots in the morning or taking notes on paper whilst on the phone to a client because the IT application cannot be relied upon to respond sufficiently quickly, or relied upon not to hang or close whilst entering data directly. Sometimes slowness is self-induced. If you have staff who have been with your organisation for over 10 years and nobody has ever spoken to them about archiving files or email, they could be forever wading through years of collateral. I have seen some amazing and worrying staff workarounds for slow or challenged IT systems.

Maybe your IT requirements are patchy and require a creative solution to turn on and turn off performance as required? Certainly the best approach is to start with your real requirements and challenge the IT delivery team to match them. Cloud-hosted systems provide the way forward for some very creative performance matching services.

ABILITY TO REACT QUICKLY TO MARKET CHANGES

One of the great benefits of having your IT housekeeping in order is that it is relatively easy to respond to market changes by reconfiguring your IT assets – whether that means a sudden increase or decrease in capacity or the addition or removal of an IT service. Also, it is relatively easy to switch on service monitoring, once you have a full understanding of which of your IT assets deliver which services. You can track usage and collect some true business intelligence data that will reveal how your customers use your services – when and why. Having an agile and adaptive IT infrastructure is not appropriate if you run a stable and static business model, but if you are trying to stay afloat and proactively deliver services in a tough business climate, then it can be the market advantage that singles you out from your peers.

Increased customer satisfaction

Although customers appreciate good service that meets their needs, they do not want or expect to pay for services that they do not want or do not use. With good governance in place you can monitor service take-up and customer response. Underproviding is often easier to pick up than overproviding, but surveys across a statistical sample of your customers should help in this respect. IT services carry high expectations – we expect the new version of the current mobile phone to be thinner with a longer battery life and more sophisticated applications, a camera to have higher resolution than the last version and some new exciting form or feature. To constantly deliver increased customer satisfaction you need to be constantly listening to your customers to find out what improvement means to them.

Good governance practices will help you identify who is using your products and how your products are used. Once you identify a problem, it should be straightforward to work through to the root cause. Once you have identified a potential new feature, it should be easy to identify the value of the feature to customers. If it is worth proceeding to deliver the new feature, you will have the data to hand to provide accurate costing for the implementation project. Also, you will be able to provide accurate estimates for the time to deliver and the resources required. As we all will have experienced at some stage in our careers, throwing more money and more people at a project does not necessarily guarantee a faster delivery, and good governance enables you to match resources to requirements.

More sustainable practices

With a push towards sustainability and green habits, there is a greater awareness of services and their cost to the planet. This has two noticeable consequences for IT services. An IT service that replaces a paper-based system with an electronic one will be seen as good. Similarly, hardware that consumes less power or requires less air conditioning will be viewed positively.

But beware – if I provide documents to my board in electronic format only and each board member prints them out at home, then the overall cost of the delivery is higher. Similarly, if I turn down my air conditioning and run my servers in a warmer room, I am saving electricity and looking very green. However, if my servers overheat or just simply do not last as long now that I am running them hotter, then the overall saving might be negligible or non-existent.

To deliver a truly sustainable service, you need to look at the whole of life, end-to-end delivery of each service you provide.

Increased revenue per dollar cost

Good governance practices will naturally lead to a mindset of continual service improvement to drive up quality whilst making process steps more efficient and cost-effective. The Japanese practice of Gemba Kaizen uses the five Ss to drive out waste and increase quality. There are some stunning examples of massive savings in factory processes through what seem to be very minor process alterations.

The five Ss are as follows:

- **Seiri** (Sort Out) - Sort out and separate anything that is not needed.
- **Seiton** (Straighten) - Put what you need in order, so that it is ready for use when needed.
- **Seiso** (Scrub) – Prevent errors by enhancing quality.

- **Seiketsu** (Standardise) - Standardise and implement sorting, straightening and scrubbing routines.
- **Shitsuke** (Sustain) – Build sustainable practices.

> Manufacturing examples are relatively easy to understand. If it takes five minutes to sew a garment and we have thousands of machinists making garments in a factory that runs 24x7, then even a saving of 10 seconds per garment can add to a substantial gain in a short period of time. There is a classic example of a quality manager making a change in a sewing factory so that material was passed to the right-hand side and not the left-hand side of each sewing machine, to save the time used by the machinist in passing the material across the machine. You would think the time saved would be negligible, but by the time the saving is multiplied by the thousands of machinists and the number of sewing slots per day, suddenly it looks like a huge saving!

Good IT governance will help you put clear IT policy, processes and procedures in place for your organisation to follow. Also, you will have IT staff who have clear instructions and the responsibility and authority to make progress on projects and to address issues as they arise. This should mean that you will avoid double-handling work and your staff will not be frustrated continually waiting for approval to proceed. Once your IT staff adopt the mindset of continual service improvement, they will be continually seeing opportunities for refining processes and procedures. One of my clients has set up a project team to deliver business improvement through the organisational IT systems. So far the team has made a number of minor but time-saving improvements. Over the course of a year these changes will save significant time and money and will provide a better and more efficient buying experience for customers.

General workplace benefits

We spend a lot of hours per week at work, and, according to psychologists, nearly all of us want to go to work to do a good job that we can feel proud about. If we provide our staff with IT systems that support their work, that are not a cause of frustration and that perform as required, we get the best out of our workforce. Moving up a layer to our managers, we want them to spend most of their time developing the business, not chasing forms. We want them to have the tools that enable them to stay connected with their staff and customers, without wearing them out with continual non-stop questions. We want them to be compliant with company policy and legislation without having to continually seek out information. IT managers need to have tools and resources to enable them to plan and procure appropriate IT support for new business developments and to plan ongoing maintenance and support tasks for operational systems. A sound IT governance framework will ensure the delivery of all the above. And, finally, we need good IT support in place for our board or governing body members – easy, but secure, access to board papers, online voting and digital signing of documents. A sound IT governance framework will provide the assurance that security has been taken into consideration when setting up systems for sharing sensitive and confidential material. Remember, though, that if you do run your board papers through the general IT systems of the organisation, your IT staff with systems administrator access will have access to them.

When an organisation is served with effective and efficient workplace systems, from the board members through to the operational and front line staff, then, generally, it is recognised as a good place to work. To test out this theory, look at your local 'best places to work' survey. Certainly in New Zealand, I can recognise a number of organisations in the 'Hall of Fame of Best Places to Work', that I know to be running efficient IT and information governance. And that brings us nicely to the final section in this chapter – what are the things that can happen when good IT governance is absent?

BAD THINGS THAT CAN HAPPEN

When you look through the list of bad things that can happen when there is no or insufficient IT governance in place, you will soon observe that these events would mostly be linked – for example, a security breach would almost always result in a reputation loss, and a reputation loss is likely to result in a loss of business. Loss of business will result in financial loss.

The reason for considering these outcomes separately is to identify the different types of governance-related root causes that can result in 'bad things':

- security breaches;
- financial loss;
- nasty surprises;
- general reputation loss;
- loss of business.

Security breaches

Security breaches fall into four main categories. A breach can be from an internal or external source and can result in the exposure or potential exposure of customer and/or organisational data. An internal breach is generally a human resources issue – somebody has used an IT system to send something to somebody who is not authorised to see it, and that somebody could be external or internal to the organisation. This is not an IT issue unless you run the type of strictly managed government agency where taking any work home can result in a prison sentence. In normal circumstances, you are not likely to set up a regime that restricts your staff from having access to anybody outside the internal staff network, as the restricted group would include all your suppliers and customers.

In contrast, an external breach is an IT issue and maybe even a privacy issue, depending on the nature of the material leaked. If somebody can break into your system and access private organisational or customer data, then you have an IT security problem. The consequences of such a breach will depend on the type of record accessed and the stakeholder group affected by the breach. Some recent examples of leaks that have made the news have included patient health records erroneously distributed via email, compact disks and USB keys containing social services data left on public transport, exposed customer credit card details and government files found to be accessible through self-service kiosks.

You might be wondering how this can be a result of bad governance. In essence, good governance policy and process will ensure that your systems are built to the required security standard. Not only that, but these systems will be audited and tested regularly to identify potential vulnerabilities. If, despite all this, a leak occurred, the organisation with good governance would have processes in place for quickly identifying the source and cause of the leak and for minimising the damage, mitigating the risks associated with the information being leaked and collecting forensic information should the event proceed to a court case.

Financial loss

The causes of financial loss through poor IT governance are many and range from user error such as an ecommerce system update that results in goods being sold at the wrong price, internal fraud and inappropriate spending on IT systems that are considerably above or below the capability required, through to poor payroll or banking systems that process transactions incorrectly. Internal fraud is more common than you might expect and, again, having good forensic practices in place is essential if you are going to be able to provide evidence of what happened that will stand up in court. And if you want to do a self-test for internal fraud on your company accounting data, and you are mathematically inclined, check out Benford's Law.

> Benford's Law can recognise the probabilities of highly likely or highly unlikely frequencies of numbers in a data set. The probabilities are based on mathematical logarithms of the occurrence of digits in randomly generated numbers in large data sets. Those who are not aware of this theory and intentionally manipulate numbers (e.g. in a fraud) are susceptible to getting caught by the application of Benford's Law.
>
> I attended a lecture by Mark Nigrini a few years ago where the theory behind the law was explained. Nigirini's research shows that Benford's Law can be used as an indicator of accounting and expenses fraud. One fraudster wrote numerous cheques to himself just below US $100,000 (a policy and procedure threshold), causing digits 7, 8 and 9 to have aberrant percentages of actual occurrence in a Benford's Law analysis. Digital analysis using Benford's Law was also used as evidence of voter fraud in the 2009 Iranian election. Nigirini demonstrated how Benford's Law could be applied to the accounts of companies known to have carried out fraudulent practices. In fact Benford's Law is a useful tool for the IT auditor testing controls and other data sets. However, the IT auditor needs to remember to make sure that the constraints (mathematical assumptions of the theory) are compatible with the data set to be tested – Benford's Law does not hold true for all data types. Interestingly though, Benford's Law is legally admissible as evidence in the US in criminal cases at the federal, state and local levels. This fact alone substantiates the potential usefulness of using Benford's Law.

Nasty surprises

Several of my bosses over the years have run a 'no surprises' policy, and it has been something that I have adopted when I have found myself with staff reporting to me. As a manager, you want to give your staff as much free rein as possible so as not to stifle ingenuity. However, staff with free rein will inevitably end up in sticky situations occasionally. As a manager, it is always good to find out that something horrible has happened from the offending staff member rather than from your manager. IT systems can throw up some nasty surprises, but good governance processes will take you down the path of putting in place monitoring and reporting systems that ensure that you are the first to know when the corporate website goes down; email stops working; all your products are showing up as valued at one dollar on your shop site; your security swipe card system stops working and all your staff are locked out; your automated manufacturing system has spun out of control, and so on.

> One of my colleagues had an unfortunate experience when he slept through a website alert that would have warned him that the corporate website that he was supporting was no longer available. Unluckily for him, the chair of the board, who you can only suppose was suffering from insomnia and considered that a quick peek at the company website would either cure the insomnia or keep him entertained, was the first on the scene. Needless to say, a member of the company executive team was woken with a nasty surprise at an unearthly hour of the morning.

General reputation loss

All of the above can contribute to reputation loss. Good governance processes will result in 'maintaining reputation' as a business requirement at the start of any IT project, and this requirement will also be a key input to the risk register that guides the test strategy. What you mean by 'maintaining reputation' differs depending on the nature, scope and international spread of your business, services and products. In the case of a security breach, would you be more concerned about losing trust, losing money, having your intellectual property copied by competitors or losing customers? If you are a government department providing services for all citizens, your customers are a 'captive audience', so you are probably more concerned about losing trust. If you are a bank, then being perceived as a safe and secure service provider is essential, and you will recognise that your customers have a choice as to who they choose to carry out their financial services.

> We had an interesting saga running in New Zealand around one of the major government payroll systems late last year. Every day we had bewildered and upset full-time and part-time staff explaining to the media that they had not been paid since the new payroll system had gone in a few months before. Having heard a number of sad scenarios, you would guess that the problems were not just a result of bad data entry and that the fundamental business rules of the system were incorrect or broken or compromised. There is never a good time to have a broken payroll system, but just coming up to Christmas must be one of the worst times.

Loss of business

Again, all of the above can contribute to loss of business, and in some cases your business could be forced to close permanently. Public memory is fairly short. If you cast your mind back to stories of some of the major corporations that experienced one of the above 'bad things' in 2011, most of them are still operating today. I think that is a tribute to the way they have reacted to the revelation that their IT systems were not as robust as they hoped. Those of us who fly a lot do not stop flying on aeroplanes after a large plane crashes killing all the passengers and the cause is suspected to be a faulty component, but we do look for reassurance before we fly again. We want to know that our chosen airline has done a thorough audit and safety check, and has 'taken on board' the 'lessons learnt' from the crash. In particular, we would like to hear proof that the root cause of the accident has been identified and addressed directly. Once we know that a faulty component has been dealt to, we might even feel safer flying than we did before the crash. However, we probably will not feel that our confidence has been fully restored until we know that the relevant airlines have adopted new processes to identify components before they fail.

Similarly, if an organisation that we deal with as a customer has a major security breach, but then carries out a thorough investigation to identify the root cause of the problem, and commissions a comprehensive independent audit and check of related systems, then that will give us confidence that at least they are taking the situation seriously. However, we are not going to be fully satisfied until we know that the organisation has adopted new governance processes and changed the way they do things to the point where the situation looks unlikely to reoccur. Whether or not the CEO or CIO falls on a sword in shame is almost immaterial. As a customer, you want to know that the organisation will operate differently in the future. And if that does not look to be the case, you will probably be taking your business elsewhere.

7 REVIEW OF PART A

This chapter presents a brief summary of the first half of the book. If you are the member of a governing body or a senior executive, I am hoping that you will have read the book this far. However, you might find this chapter a useful summary that you can share with your other board/executive team members by way of an introduction to the topic of the governance of IT and the benefits of implementing the international standard ISO/IEC 38500 in your organisation.

If you are an IT person and you are more interested in reading the second half of the book to get some hints, tips, tools and ideas for implementing IT governance, then you might find that reading this chapter gives you a good idea of where your governing body and senior executives are coming from and what they hope to achieve from the implementation of the 38500 standard in your organisation.

HISTORY

Contrary to popular belief, IT and information governance is not a recent topic, dreamt up in the 1990s to force the then maturing IT industry to grow up quickly. The principles around this subject area have been in play since the earliest days of civilisation.

Rulers, emperors, and other generally smart people have understood the need for access to reliable and accurate information to inform good decisions and they have understood the need for security to deter warring nations and other competitors. Even our early governing ancestors understood that survival and growth relied on putting the right people in the right roles and developing a strategic plan for using resources wisely. Having access to valuable information and having the intelligence to interpret it was a prerequisite for success as a leader. The same holds true today.

The advent of technology in the form of computers has made it possible to locate, store, process and disseminate great volumes of information. IT systems have quickly become a more and more critical part of all business, engineering and design systems. However, having more information and more technical systems and solutions at your disposal does not necessarily make you smarter or more effective and efficient at what you do. A group of us (with representatives from around the world) came to the conclusion, whilst sitting in a standards meeting in Bari, southern Italy, in 2005, that some guidance was required to help people make the best of their information and IT systems. We were in the process of fast-tracking the excellent UK guidance on IT service management to become an international standard, but we realised that putting in good process and practice for operational IT was only addressing part of the problem. My ISO study group on IT governance put forward the Australian IT governance standard for fast track in 2006, and the first international IT governance standard was published in 2008. The standard lists six principles to guide the setting up of an IT governance framework and decision-making model that will put you back in charge of your organisational information and supporting technology. And, like the ancient rulers, you will be in a good place to fight off your competitors and any other warring factions.

Since 2008, we have been working on a portfolio of IT governance standards covering related areas of particular relevance to world markets. We have draft standards to assist with the governance of IT audit, the creation of a digital forensics risk framework and the application of the governance principles to interoperability, thereby creating organisational guidelines for the bring-your-own-device era. As a market need for guidance emerges, we apply ourselves to creating relevant material in as short a time as possible. The international representation and the consensus-led ISO process together have ensured that our output has been generally applicable internationally.

THE STANDARD – 38500

In the sections on the IT governance standard we looked at the 38500 standard in detail and from the viewpoint of a governing body intending to introduce a governance framework within an organisation. The standard is short and succinct and designed for a busy, intelligent audience. The principles listed below form the backbone of the standard and the basis for any organisational governance framework:

- responsibility;
- strategy;
- acquisition;
- performance;
- conformance;
- human behaviour.

The evaluate-direct-monitor governance activities described in this section provide the basis for a continual improvement mechanism for ensuring that good governance practices are in place and that they meet the needs of the organisation.

The IT governance standard 38500 provides excellent guidance for the development of an IT governance framework for an organisation, irrespective of type or size. Where there is an existing framework and strategic planning documents, the standard can be used as a checklist to ensure that all appropriate governance activities are in place. Unlike other IT governance systems, methodologies and frameworks, such as COBIT (Control OBjectives for Information and Related Technology, a framework created by ISACA), the standard is set in the context of corporate governance and board responsibility and is descriptive rather than prescriptive.

For the directors of an organisation, the standard provides a useful set of questions to determine how well IT systems are managed. For IT managers, the standard sets an expectation of risk mitigation and best practice reporting.

Ongoing ISO work in the area of the corporate governance of IT will see the development of a series of related governance standards covering different areas of IT. Associated research by the academic members of the ISO IT governance working groups will help determine which of the six key factors identified in the 38500 standard are critical to the development of excellent IT governance practices. Already we are seeing that the sixth principle, human behaviour, seems to be the most important of the set. So, despite our focus and reliance on technology, we are fully dependent on the human who developed the technology and the human operative.

BENEFITS

In the section on benefits, we not only looked at the positive outcomes from implementing the IT governance standards in your organisation, but we looked at the negative outcomes that have been observed across organisations with no formal IT governance structures in place. We listed the positive outcomes as follows:

- cost reduction;
- performance improvement;
- ability to react quickly to market changes;
- increased customer satisfaction;
- increased revenue per dollar cost;
- general workplace benefits for your board, management and staff.

Even if you are not fully persuaded by the positive outcomes, I hope that the risk of the negative outcomes will encourage you to look into this subject further. These negative outcomes can include combinations of the following:

- security breach;
- financial loss;
- nasty surprises;
- general reputation loss;
- loss of business.

In the last few years, since we started work on the standard, I have seen organisations with poor IT governance models in place fail to the point of ceasing to trade and I have seen directors and other members of governing bodies face dismissal and other more serious consequences for negligence in IT matters.

In summary, the benefits of having a good IT governance framework in place are 'no nasty surprises' and efficient and reliable, safe and secure IT services and systems.

Bear in mind that it is not always obvious with IT systems when things are not going well, and the bad activities can stay invisible for a surprisingly long time.

> A business in my home town of Wellington, New Zealand, employed an administrator who continually syphoned off a portion of the larger financial transactions that they were handling by overcharging the unsuspecting customers and robbing their employer. Good IT governance would have enforced peer review for large transactions, audit and security management processes and numerous other checks and balances that would have at least identified the fraudulent activity early on, and at best (and most likely) would have prevented such activity. As it was, the deception carried on for a number of years. As a potential customer, I am encouraged that the staff member lost their job and was identified publically. However, I would not even consider using the service until the organisation changes its processes and introduces good IT governance around the handling of financial transactions.

If you are a director or on the governing body of an organisation that relies on IT and technologically administered information assets, then taking on the advice in this book could be a turning point for your organisation.

WHERE TO GO FROM HERE?

You have reached the end of the first part of the book. So far, we have talked about the history of IT governance, the benefits of implementing the 38500 standard and the dire things that can happen without an IT governance framework in place. We have introduced the principles of the standard and explained the important contribution that each one can make to the health, success and happiness of your organisation. We have looked at the director's IT governance activities – evaluating internal needs and external business pressures, directing IT activity and monitoring output and outcomes from IT systems and solutions.

To proceed from here, the governing body needs to adopt the principles, tailoring them to the organisation in a way that will be meaningful for the management team who will have the task of implementing the governance framework. Tailoring will involve using terminology that is familiar to the organisation, and elaborating the principles to help the management team focus on areas of particular importance to the governing body. Some thought also needs to be given to how the governance activities of evaluate, direct and monitor will be carried out in a consistent way by the governing body.

One final task of the governing body is to set up a steering committee that will guide you through your governance implementation. The set-up and structure of this steering committee should follow the same pattern as the set-up and structure of the groups that steer your other organisational governance initiatives. The key aim for developing the framework is to ensure that the governing body is supplied with the information in the format and to the quality required to make excellent decisions around the adoption and use of IT and information across the organisation. Therefore, to set up a steering group without representation from the governing body is nonsense. On the other hand, you do not want your entire governing body to be preoccupied by the programme of work or too hands-on in providing advice to the CIO and the executive team. They will be filled with excellent ideas for the development of the framework. However, it is essential to have a member(s) of the governing body at the helm of the group to ensure that long-term governing body organisational objectives are held front of mind at all times.

There is a fine balance, and I am sure that if you look back through the history of your organisation, you will find records of a structure set up for a similar programme that ended well. My advice is to copy it.

If you are a director or a member of a governing body, I expect that you will be 'leaving us now'. Please take a moment to speed-read the second part of the book, Part B, before placing the book firmly in the hands of your CIO, your IT managers or key IT team, and telling them to 'make it so'. Think through carefully how you are going to assign the task ahead, and how you are going to act as mentor, sponsor and management-board conduit when a board decision is required. Are you going to hire the services of an independent consultant to assist and guide the internal IT team? Your CIO or equivalent will be able to own and manage most of the framework development process, but you will need somebody outside of the team to run the initial gap analysis. The only helpful advice I can give you is to choose that external person very carefully.

I hope this book will help you towards clearer interactions with your IT team, as they understand where you are coming from, the risks that you are working to address, and the overall business delivery goals that you want to see achieved; and you understand the challenges they face in their attempt to deliver highly available, secure and safe systems in a constantly evolving field, where technology and professional practice is still on a fast growth curve.

The de-jargonised review of Part B in the final chapter is designed to be a useful resource for you to print out for your fellow directors. If your IT team are particularly technology- rather than business-oriented, then, hopefully, this book will open up some new meaningful conversations for the eternal benefit of your business.

Part B covers the full implementation of the standard from developing a plan through to execution. We then cover managing the IT governance framework on a day-to-day basis and keeping it current. Then we discuss the optimisation of the IT governance system and how your team can develop and adopt a mindset of continual improvement. Finally, the section ends with a list of resources – tools, templates and other useful artefacts that I have used or seen when implementing the 38500 standard at client sites, and a list of references for those of you eager to find out more about the concepts and topics covered in this book.

PART B
IMPLEMENTING IT GOVERNANCE

This second half of the book is aimed primarily at CIOs, IT executives, IT managers and all operational IT staff tasked with introducing an IT governance framework and associated decision-making model into your organisation. In this half of the book, you will be led through the development and implementation of an IT governance framework for your organisation. If you have skipped the first half of this book, then I encourage you to take five minutes to go back and read the Part A Introduction and the Review of Part A.

After 30 years of experience in the IT industry, I can safely say that most big IT failures are a result of miscommunication between the board and the IT executive and senior IT managers. Initially, there was a considerable language barrier between the IT people and the people signing off cheques for IT equipment and systems for the IT people. When I started work for a US computer mainframe company in the 1980s, the IT people were naturally isolated from the rest of the business by virtue of the requirement to keep the computer equipment in a highly controlled environment for temperature and humidity. Often the computer equipment sat behind an extra layer of security – swipe card access, or iris recognition (if you believe the movies from that era). Business requirements were very straightforward – we were either crunching large numbers for a statistical or financial transaction application or we were predicting the weather, putting rockets into space or trying to solve complex engineering problems. We put numbers in and took numbers out – it was very easy. Along came the desktop computer, and gradually IT went from being a specialist tool kept in an isolated building to something used ubiquitously across all departments of an organisation, and accessible from every desktop. In most organisations the early desktops were rolled out almost silently, with little training and low expectations.

I am sure that the roots of IT had (and still have) a significant influence on the way IT systems have been and still are propagated across an organisation. I still encounter organisations where the IT team have very little contact with the main business folk, and in some places there is a hint of antagonism between the two teams. In fact an organisation I visited just recently highlighted this point. The CIO appeared to be fighting a constant battle with his users. He was very keen to introduce a fully locked down stable desktop environment, and yet staff kept trying to introduce new and untested applications and generally bypassing the security measures that he had put in place. Everybody was frustrated. The IT team locked themselves away with their servers and communicated via surly emails, and the CIO escalated the issue to his manager, the CFO. The antagonistic staff escalated their concerns to another member of the senior executive. The two executives tried to resolve the problem and came up with a compromise that did not suit either party. The root cause of the problem was a classic case of bad governance that was made worse by the traditional stance of the IT team to distance themselves physically from their difficult users.

So what was wrong? Well, the CIO was rewarded (through his performance objectives) for maintaining a safe, secure, stable and locked down environment. The difficult staff (who turned out to be a group of research engineers) were rewarded for developing innovative solutions, and they had been used to having administrator access to their desktops and downloading applications as and when they wanted. There were a variety of solutions that would have worked and satisfied both parties. However, the solution that seemed to be most appropriate to protect the sustainability of the business appeared to be to modify the KPIs for the CIO so that he was incentivised to meet the needs of the business whilst maintaining the security requirements for the organisation. There were several ways he could have achieved this without putting the organisational data at risk, once his instructions were clear.

I have seen the same problem where the CIO was acting in line with business requirements, and the mindset of the users needed to be adjusted. The job of resetting the mindset of the peers of the CIO or staff senior to the CIO lies with the senior executive. Non-IT senior managers are easy targets for IT vendors. If one of the senior and respected managers is pushing for a particular solution, then it can be difficult and maybe impossible for the CIO to push back, even if the solution would result in an increase in operating costs because it does not fit with the current or planned IT architecture. A similar issue is when there appears to be a constant difference of opinion between the CIO and the users as to how, what, when and why IT services should be delivered. Also, I have seen CIOs struggle to meet the lofty goals of the organisation on their assigned IT budget. This situation can only lead to disappointment through the provision of poor quality services or budget overspend.

Thankfully, though, you are most likely reading this book because your governing body or senior executive team have made the excellent decision to implement an IT governance framework in your organisation. The rest of this book will assist you with carrying out the task of implementation. By the end of the implementation you will have a very clear understanding of the expectations of your organisation for the delivery of IT services and solutions, and your governing body will have a very clear understanding of the budget and resources that you will require to deliver them. Your ongoing monitoring and reporting activities will ensure that there are no surprises for your governing body, as your IT environment evolves and resizes to meet organisational demand. Clear direction from the top of your organisation will provide clarification for all parties. With expectations aligned, there should be far fewer misunderstandings and internal grumblings around what is delivered and how it is delivered. And once you are working in harmony with the rest of the organisation, there will be opportunities to deliver innovative solutions that will give your organisation a market advantage over your competitors.

So, are you ready to develop good IT governance practices for your organisation? If so, then keep reading.

8 INTRODUCTION TO IMPLEMENTATION

There are two elements that need to be considered carefully when implementing an IT governance framework. The first element is whether the proposed framework will work in the organisation, and the second is the organisational change management required to support an effective implementation.

I have been privileged to review proposed IT governance frameworks for a number of organisations ranging from companies of tens of staff through to companies of thousands of staff. The same basic principles apply whatever the size of the organisation. Generally, I am looking for areas where things can go wrong – where the decision-making model doubles up, where authority and responsibility are assigned unevenly, where there is inherent ambiguity or where the decision policies and process are out of step with the organisational culture (for example where a formal process is being applied to an informal culture and vice versa). So really, what I am applying is a 'sanity check' and that can only be done successfully by somebody outside the organisation.

The second element should be addressed by somebody internal to the organisation. I have witnessed a situation where an external change consultant was brought in to lead the change programme and the result was mutiny and despondency. By all means use the services of a professionally qualified change consultant, but take their advice from behind the scenes. Do not let them front up to the troops unless you are positive that the impact and outcomes will be positive. In the early days of implementing new IT processes, policies or systems, any failure was blamed on the IT team or the IT system. Thanks to John Kotter, and other distinguished authors of change management books, there is now a far greater and wider understanding of organisational change management and an understanding that different people within the same organisation might have varying appetites for change. Implementing an IT governance framework across an organisation is just like introducing any other business change and needs careful thought and planning. There will always be those who are threatened by change and, whether their fears are real or completely ungrounded, they need to be addressed. There will also always be people in the organisation whose baseline mood is grumpiness. Sometimes they get caught up in organisational change surveys and they incorrectly become an indicator for project failure. In truth, they were always going to be grumpy, whether you made a change to their working environment or not.

It is my experience, that change is more readily and rapidly accepted if all staff understand the need for the change and where enthusiastic and, more importantly, respected change champions are appointed to lead the adoption charge. If you cater for the fastest adopters and the slowest adopters, and the senior management team lead from the front rather than grumble and throw stones from the back, things will go well.

I do not recommend moving at the pace of the slowest or the fastest, and I am not a huge advocate of the 'big bang theory' unless a phased approach is too messy, confusing and complicated.

The final big thing to remember as we introduce the notion of implementing an IT governance framework is that language is important. IT people are fluent speakers of a language consisting only of acronyms. Much fraught energy has gone into emphasising the need to translate IT speak into business language, but, honestly, plain English will suffice. And you know the rest of the mantra from the revered change management books – communicate across multiple channels and check that your audience is listening and understanding. Be imaginative and identify where your audience is a captive audience. Once you have your audience captured, you just need to be careful what you say and how you say it. Fear travels quickly, so try to write in a positive tone. Have an experienced 'spin-doctor' on hand to translate potentially negative messages into positive ones.

9 BEFORE YOU START ON IMPLEMENTATION

Before starting on the implementation of an IT governance framework within an organisation it is important to:

- understand what benefits are expected to be realised through the delivery of the framework;
- take a baseline of current activity;
- determine how well current activities are serving the needs of the organisation.

BENEFITS REALISATION

Too often, implementation programmes proceed without first determining expected benefits or setting reasonable goals and milestones for deliverables or establishing a suitable set of metrics. All of these are vital steps. Benefits realisation is one of the most commonly missed areas. There is an assumption that everyone must know what the benefits are, otherwise we would not be doing the implementation. However, the assumption that everyone knows the benefits and that everyone agrees on a common set of benefits is wildly optimistic. It is worth having the discussion around benefits realisation as early as possible in the implementation programme lifecycle. Discussion will open up a number of different sets of answers and you might discover that the plan is either irrelevant or unnecessary. IT-related programmes can proceed on the wobbliest of reasons, where the sign-off is completed by somebody who has no knowledge of IT or who has not been briefed on the alternate options available. Let us suppose I lose my car keys – one of the options is to go and buy a new car. This sounds very ridiculous, but I have witnessed the IT equivalent of this.

The benefits realisation statement for the implementation of an IT governance framework should set out a list of tangible and intangible benefits – and if you cannot think of any benefits, then you should not proceed. Benefits should be about increasing revenue, increasing customer service or reducing costs. The benefit of meeting legislative requirements through the programme would most likely fall under the category of avoiding costs. Setting reasonable goals and milestones will help the business understand the progress and will keep the implementation team focused on deliverables. It is very easy for the team to get distracted and move away from the original agreed deliverables as the business sees the initial outcomes and wants to try for something different. Agile project management encourages an early prototype system, but, often, when business representatives see the prototype they think of additional or different requirements that would make the final solution more useful. This is not a bad thing, as long as the original implementation documents are updated to show the agreed change in scope. The third vital component is good metrics. If you cannot measure your success, how will you know if you have been successful?

One useful tool that you might consider to assist with the development of a benefits realisation statement is the investment logic mapping (ILM) technique developed in 2003 by the State Government of Victoria, Department of Treasury and Finance (DTF) in Australia. The aim of ILM is to prime a discussion with major stakeholders around the rationale for a proposed investment, before any solutions have been identified.

> I have seen a number of IT service management projects start off in a cloud of high enthusiasm to implement all 10 ITIL v2 processes. Two processes later, when change management and incident management were successfully implemented and well bedded into the culture of the organisation, the business closed the project down. Why? Well, the business had a headache that went away when the IT team stopped making changes directly to the live production system and when issues were logged and answered in a systematic way. The IT team protested to the business, and the business asked to see concrete evidence of what had been the expectations of what can be delivered. But in their enthusiasm to get started and to save the world, the IT team had neglected to take any baseline measures or to measure progress as they went along. The business cut the funding until the business case could be re-opened with sound figures.
>
> The moral of the story is to do a thorough needs analysis, take a baseline assessment and to determine a set of metrics before you get started. Do not be concerned that the project may change scope – but remember to review the metrics as the scope change is written up. Do not be tempted into changing the metrics even if they do not at first appear useful, except to add new metrics.

NEED-GAP ANALYSIS

To obtain a thorough understanding of business needs and the true gap between what is provided and what is used, you need to talk to representatives from across the business and from across IT (including operational and developmental managers) and a range of clients from tech-savvy through to Luddite. Given that you are putting in place a governance framework, you will also need to collect the opinions of representatives from the governing board or council.

Of course, if you are the CIO or senior IT executive, you are not best placed for running the gap analysis and interviewing your colleagues. On the other hand, more junior members of the IT team might not be able to extract the required information from their seniors – so who are you going to ask? Your peers are likely to be too busy to carry out this exercise, but a peer would be your best option to drive a successful outcome. You could invite in an external consultant, but unless they know your business inside out, you will have to invest an awful lot of time – at your expense – bringing them up to speed. Here are some pointers to help you in your selection. Your ideal person needs to be:

- neutral and not associated with any of your incumbent IT suppliers or vendors;
- mature and wise enough to carry some authority;
- able to read body language and to read between the lines of messages to pick out the rebels from the loyal supporters;
- available and not likely to disappear on another project half way through.

The next few sections of this chapter covering the gap analysis are written for an external consultant working closely under the direction of the board sponsor, the CEO and/or the CIO.

Business representatives

If possible, aim to talk to the full set of general managers (GMs) over a series of two to three meetings. The first meeting will be an informal meeting with each GM to discuss your approach and what you hope to collect in the way of information and achieve in the way of feeding this information into the resulting governance framework. Depending on the GM, you may want to run through or hand over the full list of questions that will be asked in the second meeting. This second meeting will be a white board or workshop session with the GM and representatives from their team or, better still, their entire team. Depending on the culture of the organisation, this could be a short, sharp brainstorming session or a half day with a break for coffee and cake. Prepare the participants a week in advance by sending through an email setting out the sort of areas you want to cover – but not the full list of questions.

A suggested set of questions is listed in Table 9.1. The space for the responses is kept short on purpose – you want to summarise each discussion item in as few words as possible.

Table 9.1 Group questions – collecting requirements

Question	Notes or space for response
1. What are the core or key functions of the group?	
2. How effective are the current technology solutions in supporting these functions?	
3. How efficient are the current technology solutions in supporting these functions?	
4. What are the other functions of the group (i.e. non-core functions)?	

(Continued)

Table 9.1 (Continued)

Question	Notes or space for response
5. How effective are the current technology solutions in supporting these non-core functions?	
6. How efficient are the current technology solutions in supporting these non-core functions?	
7. What are the key interactions with other groups within your organisation?	
8. What are the key interactions with external groups? Who? When?	
9. Looking forward one year, what other functions/ services could your group offer?	
10. Looking forward three years, what other functions/ services could your group offer?	
11. If you could change one thing tomorrow, what would it be?	
12. If you could add on one new service tomorrow, what would that be?	

IT team

Independent of the size and structure of the IT team, you will want to meet initially with the executive team member responsible for IT, and then the individual IT managers. Remember that, in general, you are dealing with a team that successfully supplies IT services to their organisation – they might operate in a chaotic or inefficient manner, but they have a working system. In some cases you will be asked to consult to an organisation that has transferred best practice governance from the organisational board practices over to IT and is making a very fine job of governing IT. Whichever of the above apply, be careful not to change the status quo as you develop the needs-gap analysis.

The meeting of the IT executive needs to outline the grand plan for putting in place an IT governance framework. What are your expectations for how it will proceed? What will be the outcome for the executive team, the IT managers, the IT operational and development staff, or the general staff? You will also come across CIOs who have been independently operating happily for years and might see a formalised decision-making model for organisational IT decisions as a threat. My advice is to listen carefully for points of pain as you want this project to be a win-win for the CIO.

> Whilst developing the international standard ISO/IEC 38500, I was approached by many CIOs who had the same general complaint: They had put their IT operational space in good order, had implemented best practice service management processes and had a fine understanding of their detailed IT budget spend. However, they had been derailed from their financial targets by other departments within the organisation going ahead with a purchase – a new HR system or a new payroll system, say – without any consultation with the IT team. The relevant corporate team had purchased the software and financed the implementation project, but had not fully understood the ongoing support overhead. In some cases this support required specialist skills, and IT support staff and/or specialist IT support tools had to be acquired. Needless to say, these CIOs embraced the concept of IT governance with open arms.

Once you are in agreement with the CIO as to how the project will proceed, it is time to talk to the senior IT managers with the CIO present, of course. You need to present a high-level view of the project and the results of the business teams' need-gap analysis. It is my experience that the business will ask for applications, features and/or functionality that are already provided. The IT team will be indignant that people do not know that the service being requested is already provided. It will be your task to get to the root cause of why the existing solution is not used or even acknowledged. Reasons range from lack of documentation ('we did not know it was there') through to just too complicated for non-technical mortals ('we could not use it because we could not programme in html').

Also, you need to work through the differences between IT needs and IT wants. I have witnessed organisations where bad communications between the business and IT resulted in some poor acquisitions. In one instance the business said they wanted something – a new server – and that request was promptly and efficiently serviced by the IT team. However, the business representatives complained that they had paid unnecessarily for a new server, when it turned out that they really did not need one. The IT representatives said 'but you asked for a new server and we delivered a new server'. It turned out that the business only required more disk space. This is a good example of the difference between needs and wants. The business might *want* and therefore ask for a CRM (client relationship management system), but actually *need* a single source of the truth for client contact information, which could be provided by cleaning up an existing system.

Once the IT team managers have had an opportunity to digest the results of the need-gap analysis, it is time for a high-level workshop around possible architectures.

By collecting needs across the entire business in one sweep, you will be able to work though needs that can be addressed together. For example, you determine that there is a need for a new finance system and an integrated project management system. By reviewing the requirements for both together, the IT team will come up with a range of possible acceptable solutions:

- a single package that delivers financial control and project management;
- two packages that integrate fully;
- a single package with multiple modules.

Beware of jumping into specific solutions here. The desired outcome of this second meeting is a high-level view of the type of IT systems that could deliver business requirements now and for the next three, maybe five, years. The length of the plan will depend on the maturity of the business, the nature of the business, the sector and the organisational plans for the next three to five years.

Client representatives

Ask your sponsor in the organisation to select two clients from both ends of the technical-savvy spectrum who you can interview. You need to ask them about their perception of the IT-related components of products and services that they buy and/or use. For example, your questions might be around the ease of use of the ecommerce site, the usefulness of information on the organisation's website or supply chain information embedded in product bar codes, depending on the nature and delivery of the organisation's business. Keep the questions high-level – ask about generic service or product delivery and ask for suggested improvements and additional features that would help ease of access or their business interaction. Also, do not forget to ask which features of the service and product delivery mechanism they like. It is very easy to make a change to deliver new functionality and to inadvertently destroy old functionality.

Board representative

Your final interview, before talking again with your original sponsor, is with the board/council/governance body member responsible for IT. If there is no member responsible for IT, ask for the chair of the audit/risk committee or a board member with an interest in information, intellectual property or general compliance. The aim of this interview is to ensure that everything that you put in place with the executive team is in line with the general governance principles of the organisation. You should also be able to determine the organisation's appetite for risk and change, and the key links through to the organisation mission and vision. Ideally, you will be putting in place an agile IT governance structure that will flex as the organisation evolves and develops.

You might meet some resistance from the board member if they did not sign up to the exercise but were overruled by other board members. Maybe they do not see the need for a formal IT governance structure, but by now you will have some real examples of where a clear decision-making framework will add value. Better still, you will have a plan to reduce the risks associated with information and IP leakage and to reduce the costs associated with delivering IT across the organisation by introducing efficiency and transparency around IT decisions.

Need-gap analysis report to the sponsor

I am assuming that you have been meeting with your sponsor on a regular basis over the interview period to validate some of the wild claims in the information you have collected. This meeting is the final report back on your findings from the need-gap analysis.

By now you will have identified a number of compelling reasons for moving forward with the project swiftly. These could take the form of:

- an imminent need to make a major purchasing decision for IT hardware or software;
- a business risk uncovered through the interview process;
- a need to meet a client or legislative obligation that requires an IT solution;
- a new opportunity for driving revenue through an existing IT system.

SETTING EXPECTATIONS

It is rare for the expectation of IT delivery from the business to match the understanding of the business requirements in the IT department. This might sound a huge overgeneralisation, but having watched a number of organisations struggle to put together an IT service catalogue, I am confident that this is indeed the case in most organisations. The business side often misunderstands what are the true mission-critical IT systems – the ones without which they cannot trade. This is not because they do not understand their business requirements or business model, but because some of the IT use in the organisation is invisible. Or, possibly, there is an expectation that reversion to previous manual processes is easily attainable. An example of this is an international airline that reverted to the manual issue of boarding passes during an IT systems failure. In the ensuing chaos at least two passengers ended up in the wrong country.

Developing a charter

One of the key activities to guarantee the success of an IT governance implementation is the development of an agreed statement on expectations, so that the business is clear on what IT services are delivered by the IT department and the IT department is clear on the list of IT requirements from the business. I have found that this is most quickly achieved through the development of an IT charter (see Appendix B). I came up with the idea of developing a charter for a particular client, having read the history behind Magna Carta, 'Great Charter', granted by King John at Runnymede in England in 1215. The principles behind Magna Carta are relevant on two counts. First, Magna Carta enabled the common man to push back on the 'outrageous' demands of the Monarchy. Second, large chunks of the charter were copied from an earlier document – the Charter of Liberties of Henry I, issued on his accession to the throne in 1100. This document similarly bound the king to laws that effectively granted certain civil liberties to the church and the English nobility. Thus, it is useful to consider the IT charter as an instrument for 'pushing back the outrageous demands of the business'. Also it is wise to look to existing documents to form the basis of the charter, rather than write the whole thing from scratch.

The process of developing a charter will result in a clear understanding of what is required and what is delivered.

USING EXISTING DOCUMENTS

There are a number of common organisational documents that you will find useful when planning for a governance framework. These are as follows:

Annual report

The annual report will provide, at a bare minimum, a picture of the financial state of the company and will provide a review of the year's activities from the viewpoint of the chair and directors. It will probably also list strategic priorities and the planned direction and activities for the next year. The annual report is generally made publically available. If you are part of a US public listed company, you should access your organisation's Form 10-k, which is a more comprehensive version of the standard annual report. Form 10-k covers company history, organisational structure, executive compensation, equity and information on subsidiaries, besides the audited financial statements.

Before you look at the annual report for your own organisation, download three reports from organisations that you are familiar with – pick a range of differently sized organisations from different sectors. By the time you have read through three reports, you will have a number of questions and you will be ready to read the report from your own organisation.

Statement of intent or equivalent

Government agencies in most jurisdictions are required to regularly publish a plan setting out the aims for service delivery for the next few years. The plan covers ministerial priorities and planned outcomes against the agency budget. In New Zealand, this document is called a Statement of Intent and it covers a three- to five-year planning cycle. Reviewing the priorities for the future work programme in light of the organisational values will give you a clear idea of areas where new or enhanced IT services and systems will be required. For example, The New Zealand Treasury Statement of Intent 2012–2017 lists goals, roles, values and vision and describes the strategic direction that will result in the intermediate and final outcomes to deliver the vision – 'Higher Living Standards for New Zealanders'. If you were planning to deliver IT services to the Treasury, it would be foolish to ignore the goals, values and outcomes listed in this document.

Shareholder report

The shareholder report is generally a subset of the annual report. It covers the financial summary (profit and loss account, balance sheet, auditor's report and so on) and details of the past year's activities. Be sure to read the notes against the accounts as they can be very illuminating.

Corporate policies

These policies, signed off by your board or governing body, provide some insight into perceived threats and opportunities that direct or restrict corporate strategy, and the activities of the organisation's executive team. They should provide valuable insight into specific restrictions or requirements for new IT services and solutions.

Company profile

The company profile is generally a snapshot introduction to the organisation for all stakeholders – not just shareholders. It is a view of your organisation that is designed to be engaging, informative and interesting. More usefully for you, it will place emphasis on your organisation's market differentiator or unique assets, as perceived by your board. Good IT governance can help protect your organisational intellectual property and support the process for developing new unique assets.

Awards

Company awards can be very revealing. For example, if your organisation regularly takes part in one of the internationally acclaimed quality management programmes, such as the Baldrige Foundation Excellence Programme, there will be great interest in improving the company score year-on-year. If your company is in the list of the Deloitte's Top 50 fast growing companies, everybody will be energised to build on the achievement. Good IT governance, policies and processes can help with this.

TAKING AN INVENTORY OF EXISTING GOVERNANCE ACTIVITY

Before you jump into implementing an IT governance framework, you need to complete an assessment of governance activities throughout your organisation. A good place to start is to look for the use of standards and frameworks across the organisation. If you already have a culture for embracing and adopting standards, then 38500 will become part of your compliance framework. There will most likely be a manager, or even a team, with responsibility for standards. If your organisation has not used standards before, then you need to work with the senior management to link the implementation work you are doing with the portfolio of one of the senior executives. If your organisation has previously had a bad experience with standards then you need to proceed with great care and caution. I am working with an organisation that had a bad experience with ISO 9000 certification. Now they have clients who are asking them to seek certification with the business continuity management standard, ISO 27031: 2011. They realise that they need to do it, but nobody really wants to own it.

The more seamlessly your framework fits with existing policies and processes, the more readily it will be adopted. Also, you need to assess your external stakeholders such as your IT vendors, providers and suppliers and your customers. You might discover that your suppliers already have excellent processes in place that you can work with. One of my clients is going from batch processing of orders to real-time processing. They were greatly relieved to visit the supplier who finishes their product and find that the supplier had recently installed a job queue management system that made it significantly easier for him to deal with real-time processing of orders. Alternatively, you might need to educate your suppliers on what you are doing and why, and work with them to create new processes that work well for both parties. And remember that some of your improvements will result in a loss of business for your suppliers. If you have previously been purchasing items that you do not need or using consultancy services to salvage failing IT projects, then your suppliers will notice – so giving them a 'heads-up' would be a good idea.

Let us now run through your internal and external stakeholders and work out who needs to know what.

Internal stakeholders

Your internal stakeholders fall into two groups – the IT team and general business users. Unless the IT team are totally dysfunctional – and that is very unlikely if you are running a successful business – then they will have adopted good practice and they will be carrying out governance activities, even if they are not aware that they are. It is your job to capture their existing good practice, however patchy it is, and place it into your new governance framework.

Three things in particular to discuss with general business users are:

1. What is their requirement for IT governance, and how will the implementation of 38500 affect them directly and indirectly?
2. What existing agreements are in place that relate to IT governance and therefore will need to be considered as part of an organisational IT governance framework?
3. What are the current business activities around the reporting, monitoring and evaluation of IT services and systems?

The important thing with internal stakeholders is to communicate in lots of different ways and to communicate often. If they do not take an interest, they are very unlikely to take ownership, and the implementation will be short-lived. Staff who are forced to take on something they do not want to do will react in several ways – the brightest and best will find jobs elsewhere, the middle layer will try to shift responsibility to somebody else, and you will be left with a team from the least able layer who could possibly be silently revolting.

End users

By end users I mean the clients or customers who have interaction with your IT systems and services. Any change in rules, regulations, policies, structures, internal or external compliance could result in changes for your end users. It is likely that end users of government services will be required to go through an additional security layer before they will be granted access to a system that contains data relating to personal information. As a user, this might appear to be a degradation of the current service – access will be slower, and more complex passwords or security procedures are harder to remember. However, if the user knows that this increased activity will help protect their personal information, this can be turned into a positive message.

If your IT governance changes are going to change the user experience, then give them a timely warning. Do not overdo it or you will instil unnecessary fear. Make your communications very clear and concise and set expectations of how your changes might affect them. Too often we assume that what appears as a minor change to us will appear as a minor change to our customers.

To quote the World Usability Day website, which is aimed at raising awareness for end users:

> It is about 'Making Life Easy' and user friendly. Technology today is too hard to use. A cell phone should be as easy to access as a doorknob. In order to humanize a world that uses technology as an infrastructure for education, healthcare, transportation, government, communication, entertainment, work and other areas, we must develop these technologies in a way that serves people first.
> (www.worldusabilityday.org/ Accessed 8 May 2013)

IT providers

It is important to keep your IT providers in the loop of what you are doing with IT governance, as they might need to adjust the way they deal with your organisation on a business level and on a service/system provider level. I have found this particularly to be the case where an organisation has adopted the ITIL framework or certified to ISO/IEC 20000 as part of their governance implementation. The relationship with the IT providers moves from being ad hoc and reactive to being proactive and more formal. Eventually, the introduction of formal service management processes leads to more realistic service level agreements, but it can take a few iterations to balance new requirements against an existing service.

You will need to work out how your new governance processes activities will fit with your providers' governance processes and activities. Before you can do this, you need to work out how they can participate in your requirements-gathering workshops. Depending on the closeness of your relationship with them, you will have expectations of how they will participate and how much information will be shared.

Customers

It is always worth letting your general customers and shareholders know when you are running a programme that will enhance efficiency and provide a better customer experience. Personally, I think it is best to wait until you are about to launch. One of our telecommunication companies sends out leaflets with every monthly bill describing forthcoming improvements to service. It gives the impression that they are always busy changing things, but there is not any visibility of anything being completed. Time your communications well and be very clear as to what the benefits are for the customers. If you can easily survey your customers, check with them after every roll-out to see whether they think you are improving things, and you can fine-tune your governance upgrade activities accordingly. Some of our recent major telecommunications upgrades have involved digging up the pavement, and on two occasions we have coincidentally and mysteriously lost power. The customer experience got a lot worse before it got better. Eventually we will have faster broadband, and the discomfort will be worthwhile, no doubt.

> Depending on the nature of your business, it might also be a good idea to give your customers a 'heads-up' of your planned implementation dates. The bank that I use for my company accounts was merging with an Australian bank, and my account was going to be offline over the weekend. The only warning I had of the outage was a notice that went up on the bank website a couple of days before the event. The change made headline news on the weekend and that did not exactly instil confidence that the change was expected to go smoothly. Even though I was not previously considering changing banks, I did then. In these days of global financial crises, I like the idea of a 'no surprises' bank. So, if you are going to be making policy and process changes that will result in a noticeable change for your customers, be sure to communicate them in advance.

Monitoring agencies/parent companies/subidiaries

As far as implementing 38500 is concerned, you need to evaluate the current governance activity at the interface of your parent, sibling or child organisations, and to identify areas where changes could be made. As part of your planning for implementation, it will be a useful exercise to assess the IT governance activities of your related organisations. Given that there is an existing requirement for information to flow between the organisations, this activity will help define your final framework. Your implementation might act as a 'proof of concept' activity for the rest of your group. In this case you will be expected to communicate your project administration activities as well as your change activities. When an organisation makes a major change to IT service provision out of line of its related companies, the resulting confusion can lead indirectly to revenue or reputation loss through miscommunications with customers and potential customers.

TEST AND TRAINING STRATEGIES

The best time to consider the plan for testing your new systems, policies and processes, and training for your staff, is at the point where you are developing an implementation plan. This way, testing and training can be closely aligned to the expected benefits to be realised by the implementation programme.

Test strategy

A good test strategy will start with a risk and quality workshop with all key stakeholders.

First, testing effort must be concentrated on the areas of highest risk from operational, reputational and financial viewpoints. Once the test team understands the risks associated with rolling out your implementation plan, they can identify the key risk indicators (KRIs) and balance tests and testing time appropriately. Also, it is often a useful exercise for stakeholders to hear the risks stated by their colleagues. During the development of the test strategy is the best time to work through compliance and conformance requirements with the business. These requirements generally point to high-risk areas. What have you agreed as the conformance principle for your organisation? What performance goals has your organisation set around compliance?

Working through these areas will help you understand the risk profile and identify some key focal points for testing.

Second, testing effort must be focused on delivering quality outcomes, based on the quality requirements of the business. These quality goals should align closely with the benefits realisation statement presented at the start of the programme, KPIs and the key business goals associated with the programme. We often hear the phrase 'good enough is good enough' especially when people are cutting corners on delivery, but for your programme, what does 'good enough' look like?

And, finally, the 'good enough' discussion will feed nicely into a prioritisation exercise across the risk and quality statements. The programme is not going to have the resources to address all known risks or to deliver to the highest quality in all areas. The test team need to understand the compromises that the business stakeholders are willing to make in order for the programme to be delivered on time and on budget.

> In a test strategy workshop to plan for the testing of a set of new online tools, the workshop facilitator put questions to business representatives to identify the quality goals to be achieved by the roll-out of new online services. This was not an IT meeting – references to IT and IT solutions were brief. The focus of the meeting was to ensure that the roll-out of a new ecommerce and corporate information website would meet the vision and expectations of the governing body. It was all about ensuring that the outcomes of the IT deployment aligned perfectly with the organisational goals and addressed, or at least referenced, the key organisational risks identified by the audit and risk subcommittee of the governing body. For example, one of the goals put forward was that the websites would be compliant with the NZ government guidelines for delivering websites.
>
> Now, given that the test strategy will result in a comprehensive test plan and, in particular, some testing around compliance web standards, this should provide a useful 'heads-up' for the project team that a non-compliant solution will not be acceptable. This is why it is a good idea to hold the test strategy workshop as early as possible in your programme plan. It will provide a sanity check against your business requirements, and will also help rule out some unsuitable solutions sooner rather than later.
>
> The workshop produced approximately 40 quality goals. The next stage will be for all the business representatives to rank the goals in order of necessity, with the proviso that they will not be allowed to label all the goals as top priority. After that the goals will be assessed by the project team for technical complexity – as this will allow the depth and breadth of testing required to be estimated. Once the goals and priorities have been established, the test strategy will be used to formulate a test plan, and the test plan will be used to write individual test scripts.

Training strategy

A good training strategy will ensure that all staff receive appropriate training at a time close enough to implementation so that they cannot forget what they have learned, and far enough away so as not to interfere with any roll-out duties they have. Most organisations adopt a train-the-trainer approach as it is the most cost-effective and efficient way to train a number of people in a short space of time. However, there are drawbacks and if you ask somebody who does not quite understand what they have been told to explain it to somebody else, the result is confusion and staff who only partially understand the overall operation of the rolled-out system, or fully understand only parts of the rolled-out system.

One of the most important tasks in developing the training strategy is to identify the training that will be required by each different stakeholder group. You will most likely have some foundational or basic training that will be rolled out to everybody, but then you will need some role specific training on top of that for specific user or audience types. Giving training to staff who do not need it, or omitting to train staff in certain areas is costly and causes confusion. Understanding that there will be dependencies between your training modules is a key part of the strategy so that training programmes can be tailored to individual staff members, or at least to role groups.

Given that you are unlikely to have the time or money for your experts to train all your staff, you need to plan mop-up training as part of your training strategy. Identifying who needs extra help can be problematic as your staff might not know what they do not know, and even if they are aware that they are lacking expertise, they might not be keen to admit it. So there are three options for the training strategy. You can run a survey post-implementation to weed out the staff who need extra assistance, you can run mop-up training for all staff or you can provide some supplementary training materials that staff can run through as and when required.

At this stage you are just developing strategies for, and approaches to, testing and training – you are not yet ready to develop plans. The plans will come together as you address the risks identified in the test strategy risk management workshop, and as you evaluate what training will be needed for each different stakeholder group. This approach is described in Chapter 10.

RECAP

Before you start executing the implementation plan, you need to have the core elements of the IT governance framework in place. These are as follows:

- a version of the 38500 principles, tailored to your organisation and signed off by your governing body;
- systems for carrying out the IT and information transfer functions in a way that supports the principles;
- a supported and maintained infrastructure capable of hosting the systems above;

- process and policy to enable all staff to align activities to the principles;
- a charter to state business expectations from IT and information management and vice versa;
- an organisational chart that reflects new responsibilities and authorities required to carry out the principles;
- a test strategy that sets out an approach based on the risk profile and quality goals;
- a training strategy to ensure that all stakeholders are confident in using the new framework, and that they understand any new responsibilities they have.

10 GETTING THERE – DEVELOPING A PLAN

You will now have run a need-gap analysis and identified where the current IT governance activities are weak, and you will have developed a charter providing a list of expectations of the business from IT and expectations of IT delivery from the business. You will have a clear view of where the organisation is going in a strategic sense, and the overall organisational culture and appetite for risk and change. You will have identified the key people in the organisation who will champion new ways of working, and you will have certainly identified the people who will attempt to block your progress (consciously or unconsciously). By now you will be having regular debriefs with your organisational sponsor, and you will be putting together a team to develop and implement an IT governance plan.

Your IT governance champions will be invaluable as they will promulgate new processes in their own group. Your blockers are also a surprisingly useful resource as they will be the first to identify why your new process will not work. Often the blockers are staff who feel threatened by formalised process – and there are several possible causes. They could be the organisational heroes who fire fight their way out of problems when IT systems go down. There will be those that feel that a sound decision-making process for IT acquisitions will curb their freedom, or maybe even stop some of their current activities. There will also be the cynics and sceptics who have been in the organisation since time began and have lived through a number of unsuccessful attempts to formalise process. If IT has previously been the 'Cinderella' of the organisation, and it looks as though it will have a sudden meteoric rise in organisational importance, then there will be a political power battle breaking out around you. This is all to be expected. The worst case scenario is when no resistance is observed. Apathy is your worst enemy, as it comes with no associated energy for discussion or debate.

For the project itself to be successful, you need a good, enthusiastic and able team and a strong sponsor who can go into bat for resources and who can drive a sense of urgency around the project. For the principles of IT governance to be fully adopted and wound into the overall organisational governance, you need 'buy-in' from the senior executives and a champion or two on the board of directors or governing body. You will have already set this process in motion by interviewing the board member responsible for IT, but for the ongoing work to be successful, you need to formalise the link between the project and the board. This could be in the form of regular updates to the board, or the establishment of a subcommittee to have oversight of the project deliverables.

BENEFITS OF THE MODULAR APPROACH

Another consideration before embarking on the plan itself is the timeline for getting an IT governance framework in place – and this will depend on the key drivers behind the project. If you are looking at a short time frame to get the full framework in place, then you will be faced with a big-bang implementation, where you will be turning on policy, process and procedure across the organisation and expecting staff to go to sleep with one system in place and to wake up ready to use a totally new system.

One of the hardest things to deal to with when using the big-bang approach is training. Most likely you are driven by a legislative or financial requirement. At first it seems like a grand plan to implement over Christmas, or at the end of the financial year. Christmas is a problem, especially in the southern hemisphere where the Christmas break is the long summer holiday. Training before Christmas, expecting your staff to return fully up to speed in new systems and processes after two weeks on vacation, is wishful thinking. Expecting to make a swift change-over at the end of the financial year without destabilising the CFO and finance department is also wishful thinking. So, unless you are being held at gunpoint to implement a new IT governance framework in one step, I advise a modular approach. There are a number of discrete activities that need to be carried out to build the full framework. Once these have been identified, along with dependencies of one module on another, it will be reasonably straightforward to determine an execution order. You can look at a horizontal or a vertical approach – whichever best suits the organisation. For example, having established a principle of acquisition, you can develop the organisational policies required to meet the principle. Then you can work through the processes and procedures required across the organisation to ensure that the policy is adhered to on every procurement or acquisition. Alternatively, you can work through the acquisition policy requirements with each group across the organisation and pull the requirements together as one organisational policy. Pick the approach that encourages the most support and cooperation of individuals within the organisation. For the project to be a success, you need to have as many people as possible across the organisation aligned to driving positive outcomes.

Whichever policy development path you take, it will often become blindingly obvious as you develop procedure that the policy is 'wrong' in some major way. It could be wrong because it is ambiguous or wrong because it drives behaviour that is contrary to the benefit of the organisation. A classic example here is the organisation that decides that acquisitions over a gazillion dollars need to be approved by the senior management and 10 gazillion by the board. Something magic happens overnight – the gazillion dollar projects break into multiple parts, and the multi- gazillion projects fracture into a set of gazillion dollar projects. And, of course, the point of impact is missed completely. An IT project with a budget that can be funded out of the petty cash of the coffee club, to change the colour of the website, can have huge impact. So the lesson here is to develop unambiguous policy and procedures that drive 'good behaviour'.

EMBEDDING AND COMMUNICATING THE PLAN

One of the keys to embedding new procedures and processes is to identify 'process champions' across the organisation who will quickly pick up and embrace new ways of operating and will act as leaders for the people around them. Training is another crucial element. People have different ways of taking in information, so you need to operate several channels of information to reach as many people as possible. The seven learning styles are recognised as visual, aural, verbal, physical, logical, social and solitary. In practice, to be effective, your training programme needs to include visual material, presentations by the project team, paper or online material that the staff can read at their leisure, practical activities and examples involving problem solving, and opportunities to participate in discussion groups. Remember to pay special attention to part-time staff and staff who regularly work away on a client site. They will already feel on the edge of the organisation, so do not isolate them further.

> I was part of a project team years ago implementing a business process improvement programme. Every week our CEO put out an update on the project through his letter to staff – and yet no-one appeared to know what was going on when we met with them. One of the admin staff who did read the CEO letter and did know what was going on was accused of having insider information. It slowly dawned on us as a team that we were not getting through to our target audience. The final straw was when we repeated our communications through a presentation to the all-company meeting and just about everybody looked genuinely surprised. We worked hard to come up with more innovative ways of communicating. We decided that we needed a captive audience and an eye-catching theme for our communications and that drastic action was called for. We started putting up posters in the toilets and, within a week, the project was the talk of the company.

DEVELOPING ARTEFACTS

As IT people, we often talk about road maps and strategic planning when, in fact, a simple to-do list would be adequate. However, in the case of delivering a decision-making framework and the associated policies and procedures, the concept of a road map is very useful. Staff at all levels want to know what impact the project will have on their daily lives. Most would opt to stay with the bad process they understand (the devil they know) rather than have to learn new processes and procedures. And even though you can promise great things for the new framework once it is bedded in, it is highly likely that things will get worse before they get better. There is a curve of despondency and misery associated with most IT projects that looks like a skewed parabola. The lowest point is hit maybe three to six months into the project when the initial enthusiasm has worn off, the members of the project team are tired and not making progress as quickly as they had hoped, the staff are working across two systems and picking holes in the new processes, and the customers are calling in confused. At this point it is essential to have some artefacts that will get the team and the organisation through the difficult patch. Anything you can create that will help the staff understand the new processes and procedures clearly will be very valuable. A road map, plotting the path through transition is also highly desirable. Consideration of the following three questions will assist in developing an approach to completing the transition work:

1. How will the new systems interoperate with the old systems (if at all)?
2. How quickly will the new systems be fully operational?

3. How will the training fit with the transition plan? Who can staff go to for assistance? Who are the process champions?

> Do not underestimate the value of the humble piece of paper. I worked on an IT project to implement a new system for an insurance company, where some of the users of the new system were answering 0800 (free) calls and working to targets of providing information to customers in the shortest time possible. We developed an online help system, using a violet font to make it unmistakable from any other online help utility, and produced a very grand fold-out card pamphlet, with hints and tips, how-tos and FAQs for using the system, that could sit on the desk. Two years later, when the project was refreshed, the online help was updated but it was considered unnecessary to produce a new version of the pamphlet, much to the disappointment of the key users – the call centre staff. The management team was perplexed – thinking that the call centre staff would not have time to look up answers from the card. However, because the card was attractive, the call centre staff had been reading it between calls.

You also need to produce a set of collateral that shows how the elements of the framework fit together, so that staff across the organisation can see that policy is aligned with organisational principles that have been signed off by the board, that process is developed from policy and that the procedures enable the fulfilment of the policies. By doing this, it will become obvious that procedures cannot be changed in isolation, but need to be adjusted in conjunction with policy and process.

The diagram in Figure 10.1 demonstrates how elements of the governance framework work together.

Also, if the implementation of the IT governance framework has resulted in the establishment of new roles or new responsibilities for existing roles, these need to be carefully communicated. It is most frustrating to request approval for purchase, only to find that the person you sent the request to is no longer responsible for the area. It is best if staff find out about new roles and responsibilities from the CEO than from somebody's out-of-office message or from the water cooler gossip.

PROJECT PRIORITISATION AGAINST THE PRINCIPLES

And finally, to help the prioritisation of your projects, map the key deliverables from each project against the six principles in such a way that you capture the risk of not doing the piece of work and the impact of completing the work. The resulting table will provide a good indicator for what should be completed in what order. Deliverables that have impact across all principles are likely to be your highest priority. However, if the organisation is going through a high growth or a crisis situation, it would be wise to put a greater weighting on the principle that is most relevant. This will ensure that the IT team will deliver the requirements based on organisational need.

Figure 10.1 Framework detail example

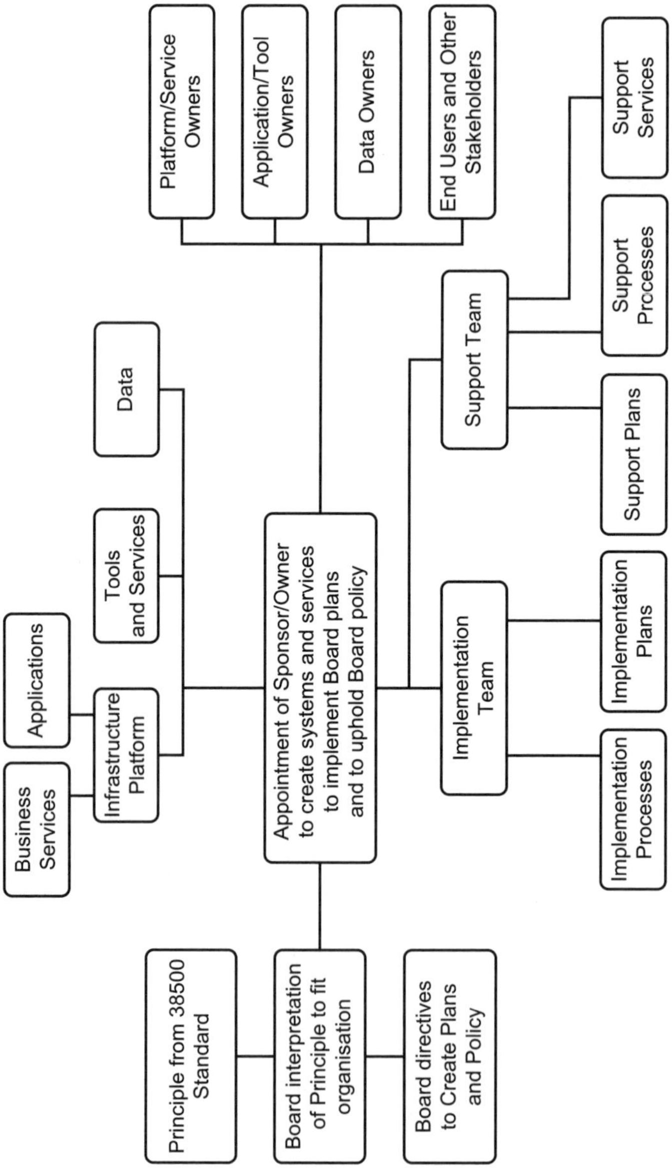

Table 10.1 shows how you can start mapping programme deliverables to the six principles. Some of the deliverables will align to more than one principle. If you mark the key principle, then it will help guide your reporting. Deliverables that align to more than one principle will be more complex to deliver.

Table 10.1 Mapping programme deliverables to the six principles

Programme deliverables	Specifics	1	2	3	4	5	6
Policy Framework	Acceptable use of IT	X					X
	IT procurement				X		
	Security					X	
Supporting Infrastructure	DR system						
	Testing systems						
	Replacement of legacy systems						
Staff Changes	Appointment of new service owners						
Reporting Framework							
Service Management Framework	Introduction of change management board						

REVIEWING THE ORGANISATIONAL CHART AND BUILDING YOUR TEAMS

As you develop your plan, you will be looking to the organisational chart to build your project teams and to build an operational team to take delivery of programme outputs. You will be looking for leaders and ensuring that they have the capability, responsibility and authority to enable them to take on the tasks ahead. First, you need to review the corporate culture and the perceived value of IT across the organisation, as this will help you determine who will be the right fit for each role. Does your organisation put a strong emphasis on hierarchy? In general are your staff members competitive? Are your staff highly networked? Do they socialise together? What is the most common demographic of your staff members?

Answering the following questions will help you determine who to put where:

- Who are your capable leaders?
- Who are your honest and direct members of staff?
- Who are your highly networked members of staff?
- Who are the staff who find problems everywhere?
- Who are your destructive members of staff?
- Who are your fastidiously tidy and careful staff members?
- Who are the rumour-mongers?
- Where are the conflicts of interest?

When building your teams, you need to ensure that your members are capable and equipped to do the role set before them. Depending on your organisational culture, you will choose different personality types for different roles and teams. For example, if your organisation is very people-focused and the vision and mission are centred on helping or assisting people in some way, then your trainers need to be highly networked people. Training can be a bit ad hoc, as long as it is sociable. If your organisation is very process-oriented, and your vision and mission are centred on achieving goals, then your trainers need to be detail- and process- focused. Training must be regimented and trainers need to stick to their allotted time slots. And, whatever your organisation type, your destructive members of staff and the ones who find problems everywhere will make excellent framework testers. Your team leaders need to represent the personality strengths of their group, have some influence across the organisation and the respect of the team members that they are leading.

The following questions around capability and responsibility will help you review your team structure:

- Do the project role names align with the staff job descriptions and KPIs? Generally, people are pulled onto a project team whilst retaining their original role. At stages of the project where the project role expands, it is wise to backfill the original role. It makes sense to have new job descriptions and KPIs for the staff in their project role. Otherwise, it is possible for staff to be seconded to a project for a year and at the end of the year they have not met their original job KPIs – and they feel as though they have moved backwards career-wise.
- For each individual staff member, does their job description match with their skill set and formal qualifications and training as outlined in their CV?
- For each staff member under consideration, are they better suited to a project role or to an operational role?
- Are you missing any key roles, where key roles are the ones that you cannot function without? To check that you have everybody you need, do a worked example with one of the key outputs, where you personally have to pick up the tasks that your team will not have the time/capability/geographic reach to do, and it will soon become obvious whether you have omitted one of the key support service roles.

Responsibility

For your team to function efficiently, responsibility needs to be assigned hand-in-hand with authority. Authority without responsibility creates a headache for the manager who cannot guarantee the delivery of KPIs, and responsibility without authority is a headache and a continual source of frustration for the team member who does not have the power to deliver their role. The following questions will help you assign responsibility to your team:

- Have you assigned authority to those who have responsibility to complete tasks and functions?
- Do they have access to sufficient resources (money and staff) to complete these tasks?
- Do your staff have everything they need to complete the tasks set before them?

Reporting lines

Now make sure that all your reporting lines are clear and that you do not have parallel lines or multiple managers per staff member.

- Are any of your teams in competition with each other? It is easy to set up the team that will deliver the 'new world', made up of the elite of the organisation, in such a way that the team who are left behind to manage and maintain the 'old world' feel like second class citizens. Early antagonism can turn into full scale jealousy and reluctance to assist the new team, if not managed well. To avoid this situation, treat all your teams as equals from the start of the implementation programme.
- Are any of your teams isolated? Though it might seem like a good idea to house your team away from their colleagues, they could become isolated. The team members will not be on project work for ever. If you intend to return them to their originating teams at the end of the project, make sure they do not lose touch with them during the life of the project. It is hard enough to return to an old role after a secondment, without the feeling that your colleagues have moved on without you.

Also, beware of housing all your business analysts or all your enterprise architects together. Your different roles need to mingle together. If they work in isolation as a group, they are likely to deliver solutions that will not work across the organisation.

- Are there any hierarchical or office culture issues? Is part of your team regarded as an organisational overhead? For example, in a consulting organisation where staff are sold out at hourly rates and everyone is aware of cost centres and profit centres, the IT team can be seen as an overhead rather than as an essential supporting service provider.

Team culture

Once you have your teams in place, you want to start building the team culture and setting expectations. You will need to put in place guidelines and policy for your project and your operational teams. For example, you might want to consider a 'whistle blower policy' before you embark on your programme. You really want to encourage your teams to report things that they see that are not right. In IT, the lowliest technician or operator can have visibility of corporate information that even your senior managers cannot see. So, what happens if your technician is servicing the CEO's PC and discovers a disk full of downloaded pornography?

An administrator is reviewing a database and, in error, he deletes a huge chunk of live customer data. He is desperately tired – he has been working long hours on another project. Do you want him to self-report his error? If so, what should happen next when he does?

I am not going to suggest answers to the above questions, but I do suggest that you need to work through these hypothetical examples, and associated questions that are relevant for your organisation, so that you can draw up your whistle blower policy before you need to enforce it. Be aware that, if self-reporting results in disciplinary action, you can be assured that nobody will ever self-report again.

REPORTING ON RISK

Most major IT projects or programmes of work will fall under the oversight of one of the subcommittees of the board or governing body. In most countries where a Western management style is adopted, it is common for an audit and risk committee to have this oversight – a committee whose main aim is to monitor compliance and reduce risk year-on-year. To align your reporting to your target audience, it will help if you can identify some KRIs that you can monitor along your journey. If there is no committee, then responsibility falls to one of the members of the governing body. It is usual for the responsibility to be lumped with financial responsibility. In the case of responsibility being held by an audit and risk committee, reporting needs to focus on the risk profile and compliance. In the case of responsibility being held by one member of the governing body, reporting needs to be focused on portfolio area covered by this member.

Keep the list 'big picture' and do not beat yourself up if you did not predict a risk that nobody expected. Be clear to distinguish risk from certainty. If Joe is retiring halfway through the project and Joe is a key stakeholder, 'Joe retiring' is not a risk, but 'losing corporate knowledge when Joe retires' could be a risk.

From an audit and risk committee point of view, the risks they will be interested in will be the ones that would stop you delivering on time and on budget, the risks that would affect the operation, reputation and financial health of the organisation, and the risks that you would fail to meet the benefits that are expected from the delivery of the project. If you start with these and think through your mitigations and workarounds should anything go wrong, you will be in a good state of preparedness for the project.

11 ARRIVING AT THE DESTINATION – EXECUTING THE PLAN

To recap on the last chapter, you have developed a sturdy training programme that covers all possibilities for learning styles, you have set up a communications plan to keep all the staff in the organisation informed across the parts of the project that affect them and you have established a direct link to a senior executive or board member who will act as sponsor or spokesperson and will shout the team pizzas at critical fatigue points in the project. You have developed some artefacts to help guide you, you have reviewed your organisational structure to identify members for your development and operational teams and you have started a high-level risk register.

This chapter will cover the execution of your plan to deploy the systems, processes, policies, procedures, restructures, solutions and so on that together make up your working IT governance framework. The first half of the chapter will take you through a final set of checklists to make sure that you are ready, with everything in place. The second half of the chapter will take you through the execution of the plan.

PREPARING TO ROLL OUT THE GOVERNANCE FRAMEWORK

On the technical side, you have a set of organisational principles approved and signed off by the board. Using these key principles and working with the senior business managers and senior IT managers, you have developed a charter that sets out the principles and expectations for IT services. From the charter, you have developed a set of IT policies with the senior IT staff to ensure that the organisational principles will be met and adhered to. Through various workshops with operational staff, you have developed a set of procedures for everyday activities. So, for example, associated with the principle of responsibility you have a policy for hiring IT staff, and procedures and forms for carrying out the hiring process in an effective and efficient way. You will also need an organisational policy that assigns IT-related responsibilities to business managers that will most likely result in requirements for monitoring and reporting of IT systems.

> **PRINCIPLE OF RESPONSIBILITY**
>
> Individuals and groups within the organisation understand and accept their responsibilities in respect of both supply of and demand for IT. Those with responsibility for actions also have the authority to perform those actions.

POLICY STATEMENTS RELATING TO RESPONSIBILITY

As new organisational policy is developed, it is important to understand the IT roles associated with the business functions. For example, a company policy that states that expense claims are to be processed within five days of receipt has implications for the business managers in finance and for the IT managers who run the finance system. A company policy that determines that bonuses will be paid to staff who use up their leave allocation each year needs to be monitored and managed from the IT side and implemented on the business side. The implications of policy relating to legislation need to be fully understood from an IT viewpoint.

In New Zealand we have a Public Records Act (PRA), which

> establishes a recordkeeping framework, and focuses on supporting good recordkeeping in government. The PRA requires government organisations to create and maintain records and to dispose of them in accordance with the authority of the chief archivist. Good recordkeeping is simply good business practice and is an essential part of efficient government. Good recordkeeping supports day-to-day operations and enables the efficient management, retrieval and disposal of government information.
> (Summary of the purpose of the New Zealand Public Records Act 2005)

The PRA has policy implications for business managers and IT managers around storing, deleting, maintaining, archiving and restoring information held in electronic format. It also poses some interesting questions around long-term electronic data storage, which are outside the scope of this book. For further reading, track the progress of any local group that have an archive function and see how they are handling media types.

Process checklists

Policy, process and procedure should go hand-in-hand to create an internal compliance framework that ensures everything that happens within your organisation is in line with board requirements for efficiency, effectiveness and legislative compliance. Not all your staff members will be process-minded. In fact, some of them will be so hazy on policy and process, or so easily distracted or forgetful, that you will be left wondering how they manage to catch a train to work in the morning. Others (your anarchists and your test team) will be intent on breaking process where they can – just to see what happens. Your staff will be greatly assisted by process checklists that help them through a process, and some of them will need the discipline of a process that cannot be completed until earlier stages are approved. The completed checklist that says that the process has been completed at the correct time and in the correct order will bring great peace of mind.

There are several ways of delivering process checklists – ranging from workflow mechanisms to wizards, where wizards are a way of delivering automated workflows.

Workflow is great until the person who approves a step of the process is away on leave and work backs up like a traffic jam until that person returns to work. Wizards are good if you have very specific processes that are order-dependent. Be very clear on mandatory versus optional requirements in each process, and enforce the completion of the mandatory checklist in such a way that you have a clear audit record of what happened and when.

SUPPORTING SYSTEMS

The key supporting systems to enable you to implement a governance framework are as follows:

- a change management system where changes can be logged (with specific instructions for roll-back should the change fail), changes can be reviewed by peers, authorised by the relevant manager and scheduled by the organisational change controller;
- an incident management system for logging issues for resolution by the support team;
- online service management tools – a stand-alone tool or a tool that integrates into your key enterprise application;
- system monitoring tools to pick up failing elements of the overall framework before business is affected;
- testing tools, such as online tracking systems that allow issues that arise during testing to be prioritised and assigned to members of the team for review;
- training tools such as online documentation with survey questions to test comprehension, or framework simulators to show how the new framework delivers business processes;
- communication tools for developing and circulating attention-grabbing communication updates;
- a document management system for keeping track of document versions, as key organisational documents are developed.

Before you proceed any further, please check that you have all of the above supporting systems in place in a form that is appropriate for your organisational size and culture.

MANAGING PROJECT VERSUS OPERATIONAL WORKLOAD

It is always a challenge to manage the project and operational workload in parallel. There will be times when you will need to invest in your current systems, even though you know that they are about to be replaced. It is annoying but unavoidable. In a small organisation it might be exactly the same set of staff who are working on the project to deliver new systems and services and running the operational environment. Here are a few things you can do to assist the team:

- Set reasonable delivery dates. Do not set a date that is so far out that the team loses interest, and do not set the date so soon that the team is overwhelmed.
- Backfill your key resources where available. Traditionally, when the IT group runs out of resource they contract in staff to work on the project delivery. I would advise you to release your internal staff to work on the project as long as they are capable and interested, and use your contract staff to keep your existing systems running. That way your internal staff get up to speed on the project deliverables and do not feel left out or overlooked.
- If you cannot backfill your key resources, look at getting competent contractors to take on specific pieces of the delivery work. For this to work well, your key resource needs to be on the same wavelength as the contractor. Ensure that your key staff member is part of the interview process, however busy they are.
- Be on hand to help deal with bottlenecks as they arise, before the team get too distressed.
- Assign tasks based on capability, accessibility and stress levels – not solely on your needs to get a task completed.
- Listen to your team, and be on the constant look-out for signs of tiredness or exhaustion towards the end of a project.

TRAINING AND TESTING

Unfortunately for many of the failed IT projects I get to review, training and testing were considered very late on in the development cycle. There will be a number of elements of the testing and training programmes that will not be able to be finalised until just before go-live, but generally the sooner the basic programmes can be put together and reviewed, the better.

If you can complete the test strategy early on in your implementation cycle, it will possibly highlight areas where the solution design might not be fit for purpose. The test plan should be written once the strategy is in place – it will cover the management and operational side of testing – who does what, where and how. Closer to the time of deployment you will be able to write final test scripts.

The most successful way to carry out testing is to assign subject matter expert owners to each module or part of the system or solution that you are rolling out. Whether you are using spreadsheets or sophisticated testing tools, your test owners will need clear unambiguous scripts with clear expected outcomes, space to describe what happened for each test and space to mark each test as a pass, fail or part-pass. Test scripts should be written in such a clear, unambiguous and foolproof way that you really should not need people from your own organisation to carry out the testing. If you run out of capacity with your own staff, consider hiring students to come in and run through the scripts. You will need to brief your testers very clearly and set expectations as to how the testing sheets should be marked up. I have witnessed some lazy and some well-intentioned testers sending very confusing messages back to the project team by skipping tests or ignoring tests that failed.

Once testers have run through the scripts, the test owners will be responsible for discussing failed or part-passed tests with the project team. In some cases a simple work-around will be possible, but often further coding or modification will be required. The key thing here is to start the first round of testing with plenty of time to allow for further coding, unit and integration testing, as required. It is not just test failures that will need retesting – you will need to retest for every last minute system change. You might well end up rerunning all tests many times.

At some point you might have to make a call as to whether you go live with your framework supporting systems with known bugs and temporary workarounds, or whether you delay the implementation of your programme. The decision you make here will depend on the nature of your organisation and business, and the risk of going live late balanced against the risk of going live with known errors.

> Interestingly, we have had a case here in New Zealand where the failure of the delivered system was initially unfairly blamed on the company who carried out the testing. It was pointed out that the testers were just carrying out the tests put in front of them, and the finger of blame moved on to somebody else. It is worth bearing in mind, though, that testers failing to run their assigned tests correctly could be held accountable for the failure of the deployment of a new system.

As for training, different people learn in different ways. If you have the time to put together a training programme that caters to diverse learning styles, it is more likely to be successful than a programme that pushes out one set and style of material to all. If you opt for classroom-style training, do everything you can to make sure that the staff who attend can remain focused throughout the session by removing unnecessary distractions. For example, make sure that everybody attending training is able to turn off their mobile phones and other electronic devices. Find out beforehand if any staff think they will need to remain in contact with the outside world throughout the training, and put in place a mechanism for collecting calls on their behalf, or backfill them if they have vital operational roles. If you are going with a train-the-trainer approach, make sure that your trainers have a very clear and thorough knowledge of the training material before you let them loose on their colleagues.

And finally, remember to time your training carefully. Remember that organisations that train their staff before the big summer break, expecting them to be ready to run with new systems on their return, generally end up rerunning training at the end of the break. Avoid clashes with particularly busy times. If you are deploying your new IT governance framework at the beginning of a new financial year, be sure not to organise training just as your staff are closing off the previous financial year.

If you are planning to train your staff online or using a series of video clips, make sure that your staff can all open the clips and navigate to the online materials. Similarly, if all your system help documentation is available once you have logged into the system, somewhere you need some training material that shows you how to log on.

Before you proceed beyond this stage, check that your testing and training programmes have completed successfully.

PUSHING THE BUTTON

With the framework development in place with associated charter, policies, procedures and other artefacts, supporting infrastructure, systems and services ready to deploy, training and testing complete, documentation and supporting maintenance systems in place, communications to all stakeholders completed, it is time to go live.

It is unlikely that everything will be 100 per cent ready for your published go-live date, but often it is better to go live on the planned date with some minor issues than to delay the roll-out – especially if your external stakeholders are intending to change their processes and practices as you go live. The second half of this chapter covers the roll-out, starting with the most important task – communicating through deployment.

Deploying the governance framework

However well you plan, however many staff you have assisting with the roll-out, however carefully you choose the roll-out date to coincide with your quietest time, there will always be some glitches. You will not be measured on whether you have glitches or not, you will be measured on how you deal with them. As long as you are prepared for problems and you are quick to respond and you keep your users and stakeholders up to date with progress to rectify matters, your users will be patient.

On deployment day, make sure you have plenty of subject matter experts and project champions on hand, walking the floor, ready to assist any staff with difficulties. Choose your project champions from your internal and your external project team and then you will be better set up to handle any questions that arise, or to fix any errors.

If you have staff located at other offices, then check log-in statistics to make sure that they are all connecting in with the new systems and other framework elements. Also, have a manned service desk set up for the first few days to answer questions, reset passwords and generally assist staff with finding information and using new processes and procedures. If you capture the details of all the calls that come in, you can build a set of FAQs to go up on your intranet once the temporary service desk has closed. There will always be staff members away on holiday or off sick who will need some assistance catching up when they return to work. The published FAQs will be very useful for them to get up to speed with the new systems and feed into staff induction materials.

Pitfalls and problems

To avoid disappointment, prepare for everything that can go wrong to go wrong. Of course, you will have roll-back procedures in place for anything that is deployed and found to be not working, but you need to be sure that everybody on the team is crystal clear about when and how these roll-back procedures will be invoked. You would be surprised to see how reluctant technical people are to roll back solutions – especially if the solution is working in some areas and they think they can fix the problem areas.

If your implementation involves a data migration step, allow enough time to carry out the migration at least twice. Remember, you would not be moving your data unless you had some sort of problem with your old system, so expecting it to perform flawlessly on your go-live day might be over-optimistic.

If your implementation relies on staff signing on to a new system with different user names and passwords, or if the new system looks different from the system it is replacing, have a service desk person on hand to answer access problems and to reset passwords.

If your implementation relies on new process and policy, make sure you have the quick reference guide on hand for all staff, and if the new processes are radically different, consider video 'YouTube' clips to get your staff through the first week.

Eventualities outside of the IT environment that you might want to consider are storms and weather events that might prevent your staff getting to work, or might put an abnormally heavy load on your customer services, and major events that are happening in your home town that might affect traffic – physical and electronic. Of course, if you prepare for all eventualities and everything runs smoothly, you would think that the implementation team would be delighted, but if you have prepared them to be ready for anything and nothing happens, they might just be a bit disappointed and feel deflated.

Project management and sign-off – handing over to regular management

Once everything is deployed and your full IT governance framework has been implemented, you will want to do an audit to ensure that everything is running according to plan. You will want the project team to be on hand to answer questions for the first week, but soon it will be time to formally hand over to the teams who will be taking ownership of different parts of the framework. These would typically be as shown in Table 11.1.

Table 11.1 IT governance framework – assigning ownership

Element	Owner	Deployment responsibility
Governance framework	Governing body	Executive team
Governance policy	Governing body	Executive team
Governance systems	Executive team	IT management team
Governance processes	IT management team	IT operational team
Governance procedures	IT operational team	IT operational team

Handover is best carried out with the deployment team and the ownership team working together over the deployment period to ensure that the owners know exactly what is being delivered and how it should be kept up to date and maintained. Support processes are very different from development processes, so the handover has to allow for this for handover to be completed successfully.

Note that just because some of your operational staff have been part of the project team does not mean that they are trained and qualified to become the new owners – choose wisely. Successful project people are unlikely to make good owners because they will have a different mindset – the project mentality drives changing the system, the operational mentality drives keeping the system stable.

12 STAYING THERE – MANAGING THE IT GOVERNANCE FRAMEWORK

So, you have gone live and bravely pushed the button on your new IT governance framework. What next? Too many organisations collapse in a tired heap at this stage or move on directly to address other organisational issues. However, to make the most of the investment of time and money that you have put into deploying the framework, you now need to check that everything went according to plan and you need to set up some ongoing maintenance processes. To achieve this you will need to review the governance framework programme documentation, including all the published documents and reports. Specifically, you will need copies of the programme accounts, budgets, forecasts and re-forecasts. To collect valuable feedback from your staff and external stakeholders you will need a combination of survey tools and interview skills. Aim to produce a set of survey and interview questions that you can repeat six months or a year after deployment.

You will, without doubt, pick up some major errors as you interview staff first time around. They might have uncovered anomalies in the framework or they could be struggling to carry out basic tasks that used to be very straightforward in the old system. By the time you repeat the interviews and surveys you will notice that the trivial issues have gone away as, hopefully, you will have fixed most of the trivial issues as you passed through the interview process.

> In one case, whilst we were interviewing staff, we came across a member of a finance team going through the most unusual and complex process to print out an invoice for a supplier. The problem was fixed before we had completed the post-implementation review (PIR) interview. In another interview, we came across a staff member who was restricted to the number of staff she could report on at one time. This seemed very unusual for a system that was built for large enterprises. We went back to our vendor partner and it turned out to be a system configuration error.

Of course, you will uncover issues that are nothing to do with the new IT governance framework. From the staff survey results you will notice some strange anomalies; for example, two members of staff, in the same role, attended the same training session. One turned out to be an expert, the other cannot remember how to log on. What happened? Maybe one of the members was distracted by checking email or phone messages, or could not see the material being presented. Maybe the expert has done something very similar in a previous role before joining the organisation.

After six months, when you re-run the surveys and interviews, you are looking for more complex indicators of success. Most importantly, you want to know whether the information is flowing through to the governing body as you intended. Does the governing body feel more empowered to make decisions around IT and information across the organisation? Is the executive team using the business intelligence elements that have been delivered? What is still perceived as 'too hard' by the staff? How clean is your data six months on? Have you successfully implemented a 'single source of the truth'? Are the contents of your knowledge base factual and up to date?

POST-IMPLEMENTATION REVIEW

First, you need to run a Post-Implementation Review (PIR). This is one of the hardest pieces of work to get off the ground, especially if the programme team is tired post-delivery. If the implementation went well, they will not see the need to do the review. If the implementation went badly, they will be too sore and bruised to do the review. You will need to push on regardless, as this review will provide invaluable information for you and your governing body.

Here is a sample table of contents for the chapters of a full PIR, with a brief description of what you might want to put in each chapter. Much of this content will be picked up from reading the extensive project documentation from Gantt charts through released procurement documents, project meeting minutes and reports, through to spreadsheets and ledgers. The rest of the content will be picked up from your staff and external stakeholder surveys and key stakeholder interviews:

1. **Preface** – Just because you have been living with the programme for what seems like your lifetime does not mean that all the readers will know what you are writing about, so start with some background to the programme – why you did what you did. I do realise that by the time you come to write the PIR you will have served up this exact same information so many times – the 'heads-up' for your senior management team, the business case, the procurement documents, the briefing for vendors, the staff communications and updates, and so on. This really is the last time you will have to regurgitate the reason why you embarked on the development of an IT governance framework.

2. **Executive Summary** – Most of the people who 'read' your document will, alas, not read beyond the Executive Summary. One of my colleagues wrote a long IT-related document and on about page 40 or so wrote, 'if you have read this far, come and see me for a chocolate fish'. Needless to say, nobody ever did approach him for a chocolate fish. The moral of the story is make sure that you write everything that you want to be noted in the Executive Summary. Of course, it also follows that, if the Executive Summary is not a complete summary of the document, not many of your readers are going to notice.

3. **Introduction** – Your audience needs to know where you started otherwise it will not make a lot of sense why you did what you did. Many of my clients have been previously burnt badly by IT programmes that have gone way over budget, or have failed to deliver anything useful. I take a very cautious approach and give the governing body overseeing the programme opportunities to 'can' the programme rather than deliver something useless. Interestingly though,

once a programme is delivered successfully to time and budget, the bad experiences are soon forgotten and confidence is restored. Anyone reading your PIR might wonder why on earth you took such a cautious approach or why you took such a laid back approach, so providing some context around where you came from is a good idea.

4. **Business Objectives** – I expect the business objectives evolved over the time of the programme, so it would be useful for your readers to start with your original business objectives and to explain how they evolved. Also, explain here how you reached consensus on what should be delivered.

5. **Selection and Procurement Processes for Supporting Systems** – By now you will have spent a significantly large sum of money or you will have signed up your organisation for a recurring annual spend that will accumulate to be a large sum of money for the systems that support your governance framework. Your readers will want to know how you went about the procurement process, and, more importantly, how you selected your vendor partners. Traditionally, you would have gone through a formal request for information process, to discover the types of solution that might meet your business needs. This would have been followed by a request for proposal process where prospective vendors would suggest a delivery platform and combinations of IT applications, and customisations that would together meet business objectives. If you were selecting a cloud solution with less opportunity to deliver customisations, you might have gone through a very different procurement process, with the emphasis more on your requirement to know where and how the solution is hosted and less about meeting specific business requirements. If you found two vendors who offered the same cloud solution – how did you choose between them? How many of your staff did you involve in the procurement process, how did you brief them and how did you capture their feedback?

This section links back to all six of the principles of 38500, and you need to explain here how you addressed each principle to deliver the systems and solutions that create the platform for your IT governance framework, and how you appointed staff to oversee the creation and the maintenance of the framework.

6. **Timeline** – When did you start and when did you finish? Did you meet your predicted delivery date? If not, why not? If you rushed to deliver, or if you took your time to make a decision, what was the reason?

7. **Contracts** – How did you manage the contractual stage for internal and external contracts and charters? Did you hit any issues of disagreement around terms and conditions? If so, how were they resolved? What level of due diligence did you carry out on your vendors and on the contract?

8. **Governance and Oversight** – What level of governance did you have over the programme, who did you report through to, and who reported to you? How was the governing body kept updated of progress?

9. **Delivery Team Structure** – How did you pick the delivery team? How did you balance internal staff and external contractors? How did you identify the subject matter experts required to guarantee a successful delivery? How did you manage and communicate with the team?

10. **Programme Management** – How did you manage the overall programme – the programme delivery with associated policy, process, procedure development, infrastructure or solution deployment and the organisational change management?
11. **Benefits Realisation** – Did you achieve the business benefits you set out to achieve? Did you achieve any benefits that you were not expecting to achieve?
12. **Post Go-Live – Ongoing Support and Maintenance Considerations** – Since going live with the programme, what have you put in place to ensure the ongoing maintenance of everything that you have rolled out?
13. **Potential for Improvement** – Very few programme managers go live with a programme without a list of the things that they wished they could have delivered, if only they had had the time and budget to do more. This is the start of your improvement list.
14. **Next Steps** – What are you going to do next? (Once you have had a good holiday, and reacquainted yourself with the names of your children, etc.)
15. **Conclusion** – So, overall, did it go well or was it a disaster? If you started a new programme tomorrow, would you take the same approach? If not, why not? Would you use the same team and external subject matter experts?

The value of the PIR

You will, of course, know whether your implementation programme came in to time and budget and what resources you used to complete the delivery, but it is worth including these other details, listed above, in the PIR, as it will help the audience understand the context of some of your other comments.

It will be very useful for your organisation to capture the 'lessons learnt' for two reasons. If it all went badly, the organisation can learn from your mistakes and do something different next time. Even more importantly, if the programme went well, you need to capture why you did what you did and whether you would do everything the same way again. Human nature prompts us to cut corners on a past success and do things with less resource next time to see if we can still deliver a successful programme with less time and money. It is therefore important to capture the elements that you believe were critical to your success.

And, finally, it is well worth sending out your PIR surveys to staff and stakeholders again six to twelve months after the go-live date to see how your new framework is bedding in.

OPERATIONAL MANAGEMENT

Your IT governance framework has gone live – how do you make sure that it is maintained and that it is developed in a way that keeps it in line with the vision and mission of the governing body? When you buy a new car it is pristine – everything works, it is well supplied with fuel, water and oil, and it is wonderfully clean inside and out. How do you keep it in this state? You need to educate those who will be driving the car to keep all essential fluids topped up, you need to have your car serviced and maintained, and you need to fix problems as they occur. Thankfully, the car comes with a useful dashboard of instruments to provide information on essential fluids, internal and external lighting, speed and distance travelled, and warning lights to help with these normal operations and to indicate when maintenance is required, and we have license schemes to identify those who are qualified to drive.

How does this all relate to maintaining an IT governance framework? You will want to be sure that you are handing over the framework to new owners who are qualified to operate and maintain it. If the new owners do not maintain it and keep it fuelled with up-to-date policies and processes, it will degrade and become useless. The equivalent of the annual car service and maintenance inspection can be provided through IT audit, carried out from the governance layer through to the operational layer.

The equivalent of joining a roadside assistance organisation is the setting up of service level agreements with your key suppliers and delivery partners, ensuring that you will get assistance as and when required.

And, most importantly, you need to listen to the requirements of your governing body and add to the framework to deliver new functionality to continue to meet the vision and mission of your organisation as the organisational needs evolve and develop. Just like the new owners of the car, the new owners of your governance framework will benefit greatly from a dashboard providing usage and maintenance information.

Finally, you will need a business development or service improvement team to be watching out for new requirements and to work with the operational team to deliver new or enhanced functionality.

To ensure that the handover is successful, you need to:

1. maintain awareness and acceptance;
2. set agreements with business, board and management;
3. align vendor agreements;
4. develop a communication and meeting structure.

Maintaining awareness and acceptance

Maintaining awareness and acceptance is more dependent on the success of your organisational change programme than the benefits of your new framework. In fact, the more effective your new framework, the more the responsibility and burden will be felt by your staff. Maybe they are now sharing information that they used to keep to themselves within a spreadsheet on their desktop. Knowledge is power, and they maybe feel they have lost some of their power by making their information widely available. Also, it is far more obvious now if their information is incorrect, or if they only have two clients and not 20 like everybody else. If part of your framework includes the introduction of an electronic time sheeting system, it will become very clear who arrives late and leaves early. Ironically, it will not be your old lags who have always arrived at 10 a.m. and gone home at 4 p.m. who will be most concerned about this – it will be your young parents who were in late once last month because an offspring threw up in the car on the way to school, and now they are afraid they are going to lose their job because it is obvious that they are not reliable. In summary, there will be a number of staff with a vested subconscious interest in seeing the new framework fail, unless you put some protective measures in place. Protective measures could include developing a new set of KPIs for these staff, so that they are incentivised to embrace the framework. Make it as easy as possible for your staff to adapt to the new ways of working, by thinking it through from the viewpoint of your staff, not from the viewpoint of the programme. It is also advisable to reinforce your IT usability policy, stressing the consequences of unauthorised access to or use of information. How you will do this will depend entirely on your organisational culture and the level of change experienced by individuals within your organisation.

Once your protective measures are in place, you can focus on maintaining awareness. Your biggest allies are your project champions and subject matter experts who helped you with the roll-out. You will know by now, from your PIR survey results, which of your project champions and subject matter experts were really helpful with staff and who was always available when required. Use these people to form the foundation of your awareness programme. Keep them fed with system updates, help and tips on the new systems you have rolled out. Send them off to conferences, enrol them in user groups and put them on the policy planning group. Encourage them to distribute information in whatever form or media type their internal groups find useful (as long as it is in line with the corporate communications policy). Pay attention to the suggestions and ideas that they come up with – keep them encouraged.

In parallel, you need to put together an empowered service desk team that will fix issues as they arise, and you need to brief them very carefully as to how they should respond to requests. Staff get very frustrated with a new system that does not allow them to complete a task that was easy to access and complete in the old system. However, if you took the opportunity to revise your security settings as part of the framework roll-out, then it could be that some of your staff no longer have access to areas of the IT systems that they used to see. You would not want your service desk team to change security settings without first checking with your security manager. Deal with capacity and performance issues very quickly. Once a new system gets a bad name for being slow or difficult, it is difficult to shift.

Finally, ensure that your staff are incentivised directly through their key performance goals to embrace the new system. If you are the sort of organisation that enjoys and responds well to internal competition, then award prizes for producing artefacts of useful business intelligence.

Setting agreements with business, board and management

If your implementation went well, it is likely that the corporate risk register is now looking a lot healthier and the known points of IT pain across the organisation have disappeared. From a board perspective everything will look 'fixed' and the members might inadvertently revert to their old hands-off approach. You will need to be very persuasive to keep them engaged and using words and phrases such as 'protecting the investment' and 'ensuring that we maintain a low-risk profile' could help. Ensure that the channels of communication remain open with strategy and policy flowing down from the governing body, and proposals, performance and monitoring information passing back up to the governing body. Now is the time to set up an agreement that states how the board–management IT governance relationship will develop. You might want to formalise this two-way flow of information, and expectations from the governing body and the executive management team, through another charter.

You will also need some form of steering group. For some organisations, this will mean setting up a board subcommittee with responsibility for IT governance, or adding this responsibility to the audit and risk committee. Other organisations that I have worked with have set up a new IT governance group consisting of board and executive management members, and this structure has been very effective. Ironically, board members who feel threatened by the IT governance responsibility will work hard to push the IT governance steering group as far down the organisation as they can. Management team members with a lust for power will make a land grab for the group, mistaking ownership for power. So if you end up with a group chaired by the cleaning staff or the CIO, you have failed.

Aligning vendor agreements

If you are dealing with multiple vendors operating under different contracts and agreements to provide the platform for one service, it is difficult to guarantee consistent service levels to your customers. You will be unlikely to be able to influence the contractual terms of your major vendors, and highly unlikely to change the terms and conditions from a cloud service provider.

The advice here is to look for alignment when selecting service offerings and to meanwhile base your internal service levels around the lowest common denominator. If vendor A responds in four hours, vendor B responds in six hours and vendor C responds in eight hours, then you have to calculate your internal service levels based on the eight hour response time.

If you have recently acquired a service delivery platform supported by multiple vendors, it might take you over a year to fully resolve the issue of aligning service level agreements for each service you deliver. However, if you start with internal requirements you should be able to bring all your vendor contracts into line within 18 months.

Developing a communication and meeting structure

Again, your governing body steering group needs to be closely aligned to your existing organisational structures and mechanisms. I know of steering groups that meet religiously every two weeks, whether or not there is anything to discuss and then, when crisis hits, the group finds itself unable to fit in any extra or emergency meetings. As a rule, meeting regularly monthly or fortnightly should be fine, but allow for exceptions so that you do not have to meet if there is nothing to discuss, and where you can gather quickly to make a decision that is time-critical. You should always have your first few meetings face-to-face, but beyond that you can resort to electronic meetings.

Make sure that the group is set up with a designated channel, so that decisions made by the group can be communicated appropriately and input from the rest of the organisation can be fed in. A steering group that meets in isolation and keeps its decisions to itself provides no organisational value and is soon disbanded.

The next section will help you set up the reports, processes, tools, structures and agreements to ensure that your IT governance framework continues to deliver accurate and timely information to guide organisational decision making, and to support the smooth operation of IT-enabled business and manufacturing systems.

MEASUREMENT, MONITORING AND REPORTING

If you do not monitor it, you cannot measure it and if you cannot measure it, you cannot report on it. Generally, if you have oversight of IT and you cannot report on it, your days as an employee are numbered. I spoke to a troubled CIO who had inherited a set of badly integrated systems combined with a set of inadequate processes and policies, and he could not report accurately on anything. He had a year of data cleansing, consolidation and business process mapping ahead of him. By setting up your measurement and monitoring processes, and producing a range of reports to suit different roles across the business, you will be able to ensure that you keep your IT and information systems, policy and procedures in a healthy and aligned state.

> Feedback is essential here. I came across an example of an organisation that was putting in a number of programmes to build sustainable practices. Staff were encouraged to recycle using different coloured boxes on their desks to collect different types of materials. At night though, the cleaners would empty all the little containers into black dustbin bags and everything ended up in landfill. Once feedback was provided to the cleaners, everything was processed as intended. You will need to close the loop of measurement, monitoring and reporting to ensure that all feedback is addressed.

Measurement and monitoring

The following are the key areas of measurement and monitoring to ensure that your reports will be accurate and will help steer the organisation. You will need to initiate:

- **controls** – areas where you can adjust your framework to meet the requirements of the business environment;
- **measures and metrics** – to link your framework to business goals, the organisational vision and mission, key business goals and key performance indicators;
- **administration databases** – to keep a log of activities and progress towards meeting organisational goals.

With the above in place, you will be able to publish:

- **management information** – by collecting suitable data and inputs for a management dashboard view;
- **operational information** – by setting up triggers to capture capacity and performance data;
- **employee information** – by collecting information from staff and providing feedback to staff to ensure that the correct information is collected;

- **board information (governance reporting)** – by creating simple, clear and concise reporting information for your governing body, using information collected through operational triggers and the management dashboard. Do not confuse simple and stupid. Your board are busy people and they need information to be published in an easy-to-read format, but that does not mean that the information needs to be dumbed down.

Reporting

First, I will admit to not being a fan of traffic light reporting. How is it that so many projects run with green traffic lights right up until the week before delivery and then everything turns red?

We are reporting on a journey, not carrying out a spot check. We want to know if the bad things are getting better or getting worse. Where I have been in organisations that have insisted on using traffic lights, I have added a second, lighter-coloured amber. The two ambers reflect 'situation failing' or 'situation coming right'. A report that says 'conformance is coming right' is more reassuring than 'we are almost compliant'.

Although the recommendation with measuring and monitoring is to start by collecting data on everything that moves and gradually work out which data is useful and which data can be dropped from the collection regime, the recommendation for producing reports is the exact opposite. Start with very few, basic reports and add information as requested by the report users. Here is my suggestion for an initial set of basic reports that should be tailored to fit your organisational reporting templates:

Maintenance report – A dashboard report for operational staff. I am a big fan of interactive cascading balanced score cards for operational reports, where I can keep drilling down from failed service to failed systems to specific failed system all the way through to failed components.

Management report – A dashboard report for managers. If you are using cascading balanced score cards for your operational reporting, it would be worth considering extending this for your management reporting.

CIO report – A report harmonising operational and management information with the key business indicators.

Board report – A report showing the harmonised operational and management summary information against the six principles of 38500, enabling the governing body to review assessment criteria at an interval appropriate for the static/dynamic nature of the organisation (see Appendix A).

STANDARDS, TEMPLATES, GUIDELINES, CHECKLISTS

The more consistent your reporting, the easier it will be for your governing body to watch for trends and patterns. To drive consistency, you will need to develop internal standards around how and when information is collected. Templates are useful to make sure that the information collected is at the right level of detail. Also, it is easier for your teams to complete templates than to write reports from scratch. Guidelines for filling in the templates will make the job even easier for everyone.

Checklists are really for your benefit – to ensure that the list of reporting requirements is met, to keep track of which reports are considered useful and which are not, to keep track of who is reporting on what and when, to collect management and governing body response to reports, to identify tools that will improve your reporting and to identify gaps in the reporting.

13 MOVING FORWARD – OPTIMISING THE IT GOVERNANCE FRAMEWORK

As always, the advice is to start with the optimisation frameworks that are currently being used in your organisation. If you are not currently using any frameworks or if you are using a multitude of different frameworks, you have the opportunity to select a framework that best meets your needs. You are not bound to select one particular framework. Choose your framework carefully and test it out before trying to evangelise your peers and colleagues. If your chosen framework involves some form of certification or accreditation, check out that the badge you are seeking is worth getting and means something to your industry sector.

Given the plethora of frameworks, schemes and standards at your disposal, you might be at a loss as to where to start. If so, I suggest you find two or three organisations who seem to run efficiently and who have a great customer service culture (because that reflects an organisational mindset of continual service improvement) and see what they do in this space. My picks in New Zealand would be Air New Zealand, Z Energy and Icebreaker. Now, I do not know what frameworks they use behind the scenes, but I would be keen to find out, if I were looking for a framework to implement. These organisations all have the following in common:

- They all exhibit excellent service management.
- They run efficiently.
- They are a pleasure to do business with.
- They are very quick to address customer feedback and to handle issues.
- They do not appear to suffer IT outages or slow IT systems.

FRAMEWORKS, STANDARDS AND METHODOLOGIES

Frameworks are good for internal use, but adopting a framework does not say anything in particular. For example, I can tell you that I have adopted ITIL, and actually I might only have implemented one or two processes. Even with the one or two processes that I have implemented, you cannot gauge how good I am at doing them. That said, frameworks are excellent stepping-stones towards standardisation and particularly useful as guidelines. COBIT is an excellent tool to use for developing solid operational processes that will help you build a consistent governance framework, by aligning IT, IT processes and business goals. It has been used widely in the US to assist with meeting Sarbanes–Oxley compliance.

Compared to frameworks, standards offer more certainty and are useful for proving your internal achievements to the outside world. For example, if I say that I am certified to ISO/IEC 20000, then you can read the standard and know the minimum I would have had to have done to achieve certification. When we first published the 20000 standard back in 2005, it consisted of two parts only – the description of IT service management as a list of requirements that could be certified, and a volume on guidance for meeting the certification requirements. Since then parts have been added to cover scope definition, a process assessment model in line with ISO/IEC 15504 and an exemplar implementation plan. At the time of writing there are another six parts in the pipeline to cover the application of the principles of IT service management to cloud computing, alignment to the quality management standards and so on.

Certification can also help with compliance if the certification body is recognised as a quality institution, if the area of certification is relevant and if the certification is current. If your certification requirements are aligned fully or in part to your legislative requirements, you should be able to prove compliance with little or no additional work. Certification can also give you a head start on your competitors in a tender process, if it proves beyond doubt that you are capable of an activity without having to pull out case studies, reference sites and so on.

Other standards to consider for inclusion in your IT governance framework are the information security management standards (the 27000 series), the business continuity planning standard (ISO 27031) and the risk management standard (ISO 31000). Certification to any of the standards mentioned in this section will assist with discharging the 38500 conformance requirements.

If you have adopted a standard and you are pursuing continual service improvement, then a capability maturity model, such as CMMi (Capability Maturity Model Integration) could prove very useful as a framework to help you work towards process efficiency in a consistent way across your organisation. I am a big fan of CMMi, as it is relatively easy to map your organisation against the framework, and once you have mapped it, there is clear guidance as to how you might proceed to the next level of maturity. The related People CMM is one of the few frameworks that address the development of your people in any depth. Given that the human behaviour principle now seems to be the most important of the six governance principles, it is worth looking into a methodology that helps you develop your staff, helps you evaluate how well you use your staff and assists with integrating the competence growth of your staff with your process improvement programme. My colleagues and I have had the pleasure of mentoring a number of start-up CEOs, CIOs and IT programme and project managers in the last few years, and it has given us great pleasure to see how they have stepped up once they have been trained and feel they have the confidence to attempt tasks that were previously beyond them. Developing the staff you have is generally so much easier and more cost-effective than replacing them with new and more highly skilled staff.

> There are some excellent methodologies that you will find described in various books. I have found the books *Gemba Kaizen: A Commonsense Low Cost Approach to Management* (Imai 1997) and *The Toyota Way* (Liker 2003) invaluable for providing guidance around the area of quality management and building a mindset of

> continual service improvement. At first, the manufacturing examples might not seem appropriate, but the principles of building repeatable processes, fixing problems by looking at the root cause and endeavouring to save time and money through efficiency without losing sight of quality can be successfully applied in the IT realm.

MOVING FORWARD WITHOUT MOVING BACKWARD

Of course, not all your efforts at introducing greater efficiencies will result in improvement. Some of your schemes and programmes will go wrong to the point where they could result in a loss of business. One of my favourite books is *Management of the Absurd* by Richard Farson (1997). To quote the foreword of the book, 'In his easygoing, anecdotal way, he [Richard] emphasizes the inevitability of unintended outcomes, paradoxical coincidences, and unknowable realities in human affairs'. Richard Farson is a psychologist, educator and former CEO and his insight into why we often achieve the very opposite of what we are trying to achieve is very thought-provoking – and actually very comforting if you have discovered a number of unintended or unexpected outcomes at the end of your programme.

How will you know if your efforts to improve your business have backfired, and what will you do about it? How will you identify and measure the unexpected benefits? Some negative consequences are temporary. Suppose I revamp my ecommerce site and provide more detail on my products so that my customers do not buy the wrong item by mistake. Well, initially, I might appear to lose sales, but eventually my number of repeat customers should increase.

Critical success factors and critical failure factors

What does success look like? Have you planned and prepared for success? What would failure look like? Ironically, it is easier to prepare for failure and to set up reward schemes that inadvertently encourage failure. Are you rewarding your team based on success or failure? If they are enjoying being part of a programme team and you have taken them away from the burden of responsibility of a less interesting operational job, then success to them might look like keeping the programme going for as long as possible. You might find that your career-minded team members are more incentivised by the promise of a more interesting role once the programme ends than a bonus payment. If you can promise them some sort of 'life after go-live' that involves them contributing to an ongoing, never-ending continual service improvement project, they will feel that the hours they have put in to make the programme a success have been worthwhile. Once you have them hooked on delivering successful projects you can get more ambitious every year.

Most of us human beings respond well to incentives, but often we are encouraged by just seeing the fruit of our labours. For example, I acquired a pedometer at the end of last year, and seeing the number of steps I had walked at the end of the day encouraged me to walk further the next day. My critical failure occurred when I put the pedometer through the washing machine by mistake. Failures will occur. One of the measures of your success will be how well and how quickly you respond and move on from failure.

Keep redefining the critical success factors, and get more ambitious every year.

Key performance indicators and key goals

Set realistic business goals and make sure that the performance indicators you set for your staff all align to those business goals. If you incentivise your IT team managers to spend as little money as possible on IT systems, then you cannot expect them to deliver high-quality services. If you incentivise your IT team managers on providing a highly secure environment, you should not be surprised when they refuse to support you connecting your iPad to the company network. Whatever you set for your staff will drive their behaviour. I know that sounds obvious, but you would be surprised how many managers complain that their staff have made poor procurement choices, missed maintenance tasks, run infrastructure components beyond their use by date or replaced them too quickly. In many instances when we have investigated the root cause of such behaviour, it has turned out that the staff in question were just pursuing their performance targets.

Be careful what you wish for, and make sure that what you wish for is supported by organisational goals, business goals and individual goals. I find the cascading balanced score-card approach to reporting, referred to in Chapter 4, helps make it very clear where the goals across the organisation might not be aligned.

Write very clear KPIs and list them under headings so that your staff member knows what you are trying to achieve through each goal. It will help greatly if you can suggest what the desired behaviour, outputs and outcomes would look like. As a staff member, I would like to know what is expected of me to be ranked as outstanding, meeting or exceeding expectations, developing/needing improvement and unacceptable. If I am new to the role, this will give me a clear idea of what is expected and I will not be too concerned if I do not 'exceed expectations' from day one. If I have been in the role for years and I continually deliver 'outstanding' work, I might want to look for something more challenging.

Risks and countermeasures

One of your greatest aids for supporting business improvement is the organisational risk register. For most business risks, IT systems or data and information management will be part of the mitigation or part of the solution. Keep your own IT risk register, and review it with your management on a weekly basis. It will provide a useful guide to the areas of the IT systems and services where you should be focusing your business improvement efforts. Send a consolidated version of your risk register, highlighting critical risks that affect the whole organisation, through to be incorporated into the organisational risk register.

Make addressing risks part of your CIO reporting through to the board. One of my clients moved from seven critical-rated IT-related organisational risks to zero in the space of two years through the implementation of a comprehensive work programme. It is very satisfying for your governing body to watch the number of risks reducing.

Self-assessment

Beware of self-assessment. I know that it is very popular for boards to self-assess and that there are some excellent self-assessment tools and frameworks available. However, I cannot think of many areas of life where self-assessment is reliable, so why would you entrust the development of your organisational leaders to a self-assessment process?

Auditing

Having your systems audited might not directly help you optimise your governance framework, but it will help you detect whether you are starting to slip backwards. An audit is a bit like a car service or an annual dental check-up. You hope nothing is wrong, because you know that would involve inconvenience and expense, and maybe a bit of pain in the short term. On the other hand, you would rather find out about that cracked filling before it develops into an abscess, or the soft brakes before they let you down on a wet motorway late at night.

A good auditor, like a competent dentist and an enthusiastic car mechanic, will leave you with hints, tips and ideas as to how you can improve your current state, and if you are being audited against an ISO standard, they will hopefully leave you with a nice certificate for the wall.

Besides the developing governance of IT audit ISO standard, there are also a number of audit schemes to consider in this area, such as Cobit and TickIT.

MEASURING SATISFACTION – REVIEWING PROGRESS

This section covers the area of collecting feedback from all your stakeholder groups to determine whether they perceive that services are improving. It is useful to collect feedback three months, six months and one year after the initial implementation. The reasoning behind this suggested timeframe is as follows. After three months you will have addressed all the critical and urgent issues, but you will have members of staff and customers who are still finding their way with the new framework. You can use this initial review to identify further training or communication needs. By six months everything should have settled down and the uptake on the new systems should have increased since the three month review. After one year, the framework should be just about invisible to all stakeholders in that it is fully embedded into the business as usual activity of the organisation.

Board satisfaction

So, your staff are happily incentivised to continue developing your framework to meet emerging and evolving business goals, you have completed an audit to check that you are not slipping backwards, and you are running risk registers and issues registers to keep on top of problems as they arise. But how do you know if your board is satisfied with the roll-out of the new framework? Do they now have the information that they require to monitor IT activity and information systems across the organisation? Can they see positive outcomes from activities and tasks that they have directed?

Do your new reports inform them to make better decisions both for the business and for the development of the supporting systems? Do they still feel engaged with the governance programme and are they aware of current activities? Do they see any overall organisational improvements?

You will want to hear back from your board, and the best way to approach this is via your board sponsor. Your board sponsor will be able to give you their view on how the programme is progressing as it goes along, and will be able to answer the questions above on behalf of their colleagues. They will also be able to advise you on the best way to get direct feedback from other board members. Given that most boards are made up of diverse members, it is very helpful to have direct feedback from three to four members at critical points in the programme. A half-hour, one-to-one interview slot with members can be particularly helpful when you are formulating the next phase of delivery. Note that your questions should be around the vision for the direction of the organisation, not around the success so far of the programme.

Customer satisfaction

Have your customers noticed a positive change since the deployment of your IT governance framework? Surveys and interviews can be useful tools, but you do not want to place an unnecessary burden on your customers, so make sure that any effort here is lightweight. For example, you could put out a survey through your website or your call centre, but keep the number of questions to three to five, and keep the questions short and easy to answer. Alternatively, you could run an official launch of the programme and invite your most influential and loyal customers. It will send a very good signal to your customers that you are serious about continual service improvement, and they will enjoy celebrating your success with you. Do not tell them how bad everything was before you ran the programme – either they know already or they do not need to know. Keep the serious content of the celebration to a minimum, and send everybody away with something that will help them remember what you have done.

Management satisfaction

Often, middle managers end up with increased workload when new processes and policies are rolled out. They have to keep the peace with staff who have gone through a switchover to new processes and procedures, they are the first port of escalation for disoriented customers, and they still have their normal workload to process. This is not a good time to put a survey under their noses or to put them through an interview. However, this is a good time to provide admin and other support, and generally pamper them with any remaining project budget.

The best time to survey management is once the first set of deliverables is stable and whilst you are planning the second set of deliverables. Only ask for suggestions for improvement if you are at a stage where you are still able to incorporate input. Otherwise, present what is going to happen and ask for feedback and comments. Look particularly for feedback on where resources are stretched or where there is a lack of policy or procedure to support the programme.

Employee satisfaction

Employee surveys are not always successful. A better approach is to interview individuals and talk to staff informally at the water coolers, in the kitchen and by the lift. Rather than quiz staff on the benefits of the IT governance framework, look for signs of frustration and listen for their suggestions for tweaking the framework to make it easier to work with.

Stakeholder satisfaction

And, finally, there are all your other stakeholders who have a connection with your organisation – however loose or tenuous that connection is. This is where a light survey – in the style of a pop quiz – could be perfect to gauge an outsider view to the organisational changes that you have completed.

BUILDING ON SUCCESS

If the results of your satisfaction survey are not as good as you had hoped, you have some work to do to make improvements. The biggest danger, though, is that your satisfaction survey results are good, you think you have completed your mission and complacency sets in. So get planning and book an external review and get reading to keep ahead of tried and tested practices. Find a set of companies that you admire and see what they are doing. Do not look for badges in the form of certifications and accolades, but look for results. Of course, if you are offered badges and certificates on the way, make sure that you display them where every visitor to your organisation can see them.

14 REVIEW OF PART B

This chapter presents a brief summary of the second half of the book, Part B. In this part we have covered the implementation of the governance of IT standard 38500, starting with planning for implementation and finishing with optimising the delivered IT governance framework.

BEFORE YOU START

Too often we rush into IT programmes without a pause to stop and reflect on the consequences or the desired outcomes. Often there is a pressing business need to get a new service up and running in the shortest possible time, or there is an urgent IT need to fix a major issue, to block up a potential security loophole or to replace a failing component or system.

The implementation of a successful IT governance framework will affect your entire organisation, your policy and procedures, your IT systems and your assigned IT roles and responsibilities. It will change the way that your business projects involving an IT element (which will be most of your business projects) are delivered from now onwards. Not only does the implementation need some careful planning, but you need to have a very clear view of the expected outcomes and benefits before you start.

You have the standard and you have a view from your governing body as to how they interpret the six principles for your organisation. In Chapter 9 we looked at how you can gain a clear understanding of the expected benefits from working on a comprehensive set of benefits realisation statements with your board sponsor and senior executives.

Before you start on implementation, we identified that you need a very clear idea of the status quo – an evaluation of current governance and related activities. This information, together with the work you have done with the executive and leadership teams on expected benefits, will enable you to put together a gap analysis and to identify areas where work needs to be done to implement the framework.

And, finally, this chapter covered the development of test and training strategies that align with the benefits statements and desired outcomes from your IT governance framework implementation programme. We looked at how bucking the trend, and not leaving testing and training to the last minute in your implementation plan, would help support quality outputs and outcomes.

GETTING THERE

Chapter 10 is all about developing your implementation plan. We looked at how you should proceed, collecting useful artefacts on the way, to ensure that your plan is fully aligned with the organisational goals, and that it will proceed in a way that is acceptable in your organisational culture. We looked at building the plan, assigning roles, evaluating your supporting systems and building the implementation team.

ARRIVING AT THE DESTINATION

By the time you have worked through the book this far you will have a plan to deploy the systems, processes, policies, procedures, restructures, solutions, and so on that together make up your working IT governance framework. In Chapter 11 we worked through a set of checklists to make sure that you have everything in place, and then we looked at the execution of the plan. And, once the framework was deployed, we looked at the final handover tasks of the implementation team.

STAYING THERE

In Chapter 12 we covered the writing up of the dreaded Post Implementation Review (PIR) and using the output of the review to fine-tune the framework and set up maintenance and monitoring processes.

MOVING FORWARD

Finally we looked at optimising your governance framework to ensure that it evolves in line with the organisation to continue to deliver significant benefits. Chapter 13 covered how to get the most value out of assessments and surveys and how to establish measurement methods and organisational expectations to ensure that you continue to build on your success.

WHERE TO FROM HERE?

If you are a member of the IT team tasked with implementing the 38500 standard, I hope you have found this part of the book useful. If you have not already, I encourage you to read the first part of the book – Part A – Introduction to the Governance of IT – or at least the Part A review in Chapter 7.

If you are member of a governing body or a senior executive, you will find that this chapter gives you a good summary of how your CIO, IT executives and IT team could approach the implementation of an IT governance framework based on the 38500 standard.

How you proceed from here depends very much on the nature, type and size of your organisation and how your governing body operates and interacts with your management team. So, once you are ready to proceed with the implementation of an IT governance framework aligned with the ISO standard 38500, and there is a clear understanding of what needs to be achieved, get started! Organisations with good governance practices are more successful than those without. What are you waiting for?

APPENDIX A
THE BOARD REPORT

Alas, there is no 'one-size-fits-all' report that will work perfectly for all governing bodies. The type and length and format of the report will differ depending on the size and culture of the organisation, and the nature of your business and the perceived dependency on IT systems. By way of consolation, here are some questions to assist you with developing a suitable report for your organisation, assuming that you are starting from scratch and that you are not currently reporting through to the board.

First, you need your board sponsor to suggest the favoured presentation format for reports and the favoured way of viewing papers: online on a screen (for viewing on a desktop, smart phone or on a tablet), and/or printed (colour or black and white, and landscape or portrait format)? Do the board prefer data presented as spreadsheets (lots of numbers) or as pie charts (graphical view of data)?

Once you have these questions answered, and you have seen an exemplar board paper to work with, you will be ready to put something together.

Your one-page summary for your graphically minded board could be a set of pie charts showing your financial position, risks and risk classifications, performance information across your IT-enabled services, and a timeline showing planned deployments for major projects. If you have a spreadsheet-minded board, then you will most likely find that they do not feel that they require a one page graphical summary, but keep the report as short as possible.

The board will want a straight-forward, clear presentation of the facts, but remember that the information does not need to be dumbed down to fit on the page, and it is possible to present complex data in a clear format.

Generally (and we are talking very generally here), the board will want to see an IT update on:

- the financial situation (P&L, actual vs. budget, cash flow, capital expenditure and so on);
- stakeholders (personnel, internal and external customers and users);
- performance, availability and continuity of services and capacity planning;
- legislative considerations (licensing, compliance requirements and so on);
- risks, and security and privacy considerations;

- strategy and planning in progress with associated forecast budgets and in line with technology trends;
- major programmes in development and major programmes that have just gone into production.

As you can see from the above list, it should be relatively easy to report against the six principles listed in 38500 and to provide supporting graphs or spreadsheets so that the board can build up a pattern of activity and can identify progress across the different areas. Use the principle names as headings for your report and everything should fall into place nicely.

Do not fall into the trap of making each report look like the report before to the point where you omit to report on annual or infrequent activities, such as your disaster recovery exercise.

CASCADING BALANCED SCORE CARD EXAMPLE

The balanced score card traditionally groups four types of activities for reporting purposes, so pick four areas that are most pertinent to the running of your organisation, or try and bundle the six principles across four headings as I have below.

Starting from the top – identify what the board want to see. Now work out what data has to be collected at the management layer to provide this information. Now we know what the management layer need to report on, we can work out what data needs to be collected at the operational layer. The resulting cascading score cards could look something like Figure A.1:

GOVERNANCE OF IT

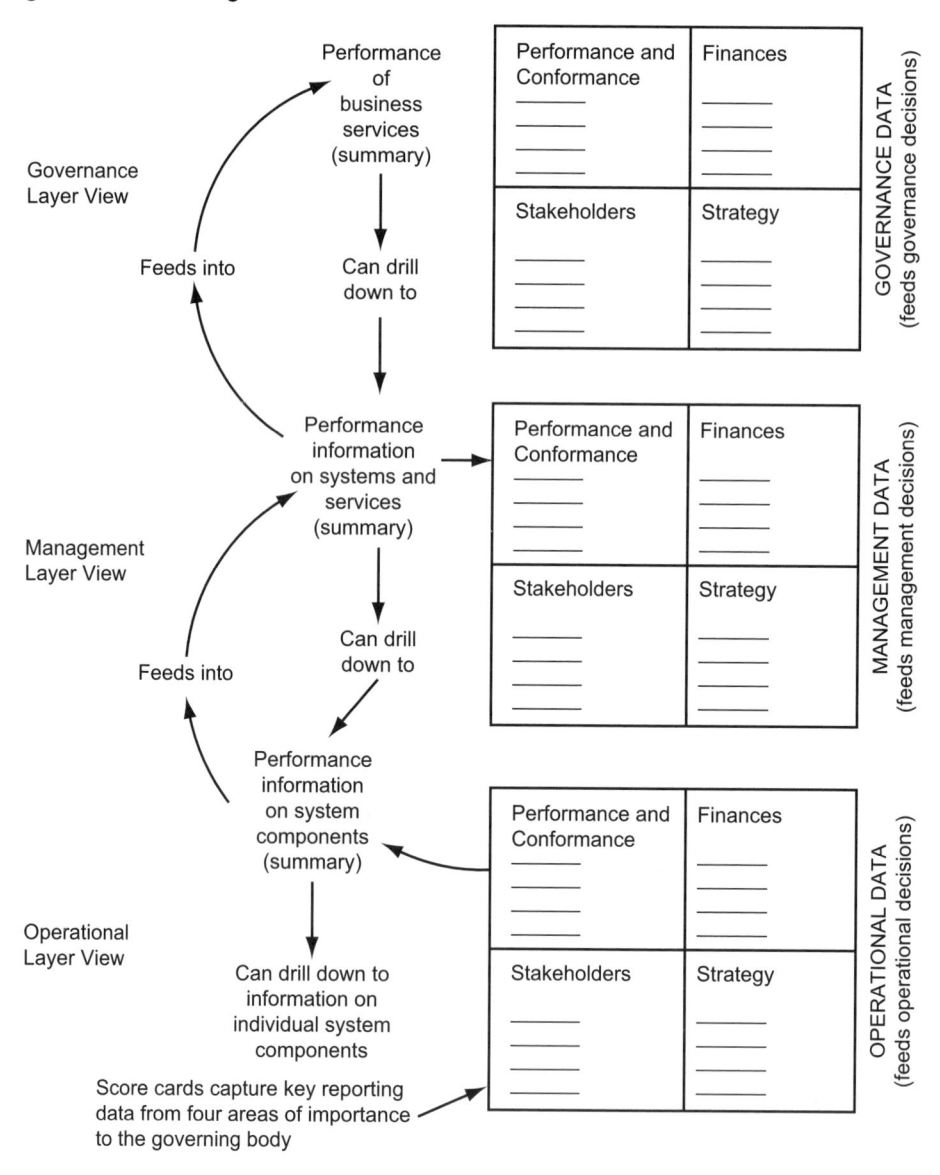

Figure A.1 Cascading balanced score cards in action

APPENDIX B
CHARTER EXAMPLE

The aim of a charter between IT and the rest of the business is to ensure that there is a clear understanding of what will be delivered, and how and when it will be delivered. There is a growing trend to make IT systems configurable such that end users in the business can make changes to how their applications work, without the need to involve the IT team members. This all sounds good and empowering for the business users, but this practice can leave some grey areas around who trains the business users to make configurations. When do the IT team need to get involved? Who is responsible for documenting how the application works?

A charter helps here by bringing the expectations of the business users and IT support staff together in one document. Again, the format and layout and level of detail in your charter will depend on the complexity, size and nature of your business. As a general rule, you will want to include the following:

- a list of business IT services provided by the IT team, together with an expectation of service levels;
- an explanation of processes for issue and problem management handling;
- a statement on capacity and performance;
- some reassurance around disaster recovery and business continuity measures that are in place.

For each business application, you will need to document:

- responsibilities of the IT team in providing the application;
- responsibilities of the business users in using the application.

You will also need:

- a change management process for business users to document application configuration changes;
- a change management process for the IT team to make system and service changes.

It is also worth capturing expectations of how training will happen, how service upgrades will be applied and when, and how conflicts will be addressed.

GOVERNANCE OF IT

And, finally, there needs to be a written record that the charter has been understood and is accepted by the business users and the IT team. This can be in the form of dated signatures at the bottom of the charter.

> Here is an example for an imaginary business service that we will call Kazaz. Kazaz is a financial services tool that helps me as a business user to work out a share portfolio for my investment customers. My customers are located in Europe and Asia, and I need high availability. From the charter, I am expecting to see processes for incident, change and problem management so that I know who to call and how to call them if I cannot get Kazaz to run. I expect to see some details on the business continuity processes that will keep my application up and running in a disaster. I expect my maintenance times to be during hours when my European and Asian customers are asleep. I will sign to take ownership for all configurations of Kazaz and to provide training for my staff and any other staff in the business who want to use Kazaz. I want to be given two weeks' notice of all planned maintenance on the platform that hosts Kazaz or on any application that integrates with Kazaz. However, I expect to test new versions of Kazaz myself and to inform the IT team if I want them to upgrade my application. In the case of an emergency outage, I would like to be notified of what is happening and when I can expect a return to normal service, within half an hour of the start of the outage.
>
> I expect to see a change management process to show how and when changes will be applied that might affect my application, and to detail how I will be consulted as the application owner. If an emergency change needs to be applied to the hosting platform, I expect to be informed within four hours of the change being applied.

Exactly how information is captured in your charter is up to you – you know your audience well. Most of your services (email, Internet, file storage and so on) will be common across all business users, will sit on the same platform with common maintenance and support times and common processes for dealing with change, incidents, problems, updates, retirements and replacements, and for providing general support, information and training. These services can be summarised in one table. It is only your business unit specific services, such as the Kazaz example, that will need to be documented separately.

The production of a charter might seem an unnecessary or difficult process. However, in capturing the deep and meaningful communication between IT providers and business users, it results in an acknowledgement of working practices neceessary to meet organisational goals. It can be the first step towards an alignment that will enable the governing body to fully govern IT across your organisation.

REFERENCES

Armstrong, A. and Francis, R. (2004) *HB 400-2004 Introduction to Corporate Governance*. Sydney, Standards Australia.

ASD Europe (2010) *ASD-Simplified Technical English* (ASD-STE100). Brussels, AeroSpace and Defence Industries Association of Europe.

Babbage, C. (1864) *Passages from the Life of a Philosopher*. London, Longman Green.

British Standards Institute publications available from http://shop.bsigroup.com/

    BS 13500: 2012 *Code of Practice for Delivering Effective Governance*.

Cabinet Office (2011) *ITIL Lifecycle Suite*. London, The Stationery Office.

Cadbury, A. (1992) *The Financial Aspects of Corporate Governance*. London, Gee & Co. (a division of Professional Publishing Ltd).

Charan, R., Drotter, S. and Noel, J. (2011) *The Leadership Pipeline: How to Build the Leadership Powered Company*. San Fransisco, John Wiley & Sons.

CMMi Institute *CMMi Framework*. Pittsburg, PA, CMMi Institute (a subsidiary of Carnegie Mellon). Available at www.sei.cmu.edu/library/?location=secondary-nav&source=156499

CMMi Institute *People Capability Maturity Model Framework*. Pittsburg, PA, CMMi Institute (a subsidiary of Carnegie Mellon). Available at www.sei.cmu.edu/library/?location=secondary-nav&source=156499

CMMi Institute *Business Process Capability Maturity Model*. Pittsburg, PA, CMMi Institute (a subsidiary of Carnegie Mellon). Available at www.sei.cmu.edu/library/?location=secondary-nav&source=156499

Dubbey, J. M. (1978) *The Mathematical Work of Charles Babbage*. Cambridge, Cambridge University Press.

Farson, R. (1997) *Management of the Absurd*. New York, Free Press

Imai, M. (1997) *Gemba Kaizen: A Commonsense, Low-Cost Approach to Management*. New York, McGraw-Hill.

Institute of Directors in New Zealand (2012) *The Four Pillars of Governance Best Practice*. Wellington, NZ, Institute of Directors in New Zealand inc. Available at: www.iod.org.nz/Publications/TheFourPillarsofGovernanceBestPractice.aspx

ISO Publications available from www.iso.org

   ISO/IEC 20000 series *Information Technology: Service Management*.

   ISO/IEC 27000 series *Information Technology: Security Techniques*.

   ISO/IEC 38500:2008 *Corporate Governance of Information Technology*.

   ISO/IEC JTC1/SC7/WG40 *Study Group Report on Governance of Consumer IT in a Business Domain*, published May 2012 (Paper).

   ISO/IEC 15504 series *Information Technology: Process Assessment*.

   ISO 22301: 2012 *Societal Security: Business Continuity Management Systems*.

   ISO 22310:2006 *Information and Documentation*.

   ISO 24774: 2010 *Systems and Software Engineering – Life Cycle Management – Guidelines for Process Description*.

   ISO 26000: *Social Responsibility*.

   ISO 27031: 2011 *Information Technology – Security Techniques – Guidelines for Information and Communication Technology Readiness for Business Continuity*.

   ISO 31000:2009 *Risk Management*.

ISO Draft Publications:

   WD ISO/IEC 30120 *IT Audit – Audit Guidelines for Governance of IT*.

   CD ISO/IEC 30121 *Governance of Digital Forensic Risk Framework*.

Liker, J. (2003) *The Toyota Way: 14 Management Principles from the World's Greatest Manufacturer*. New York, McGraw-Hill.

Magna Carta (1215) Available at: www.archives.gov/exhibits/featured_documents/magna_carta/translation.html

New Zealand Public Records Act (2005) Available at www.legislation.govt.nz/act/public/2005/0040/latest/DLM345529.html

Nigrini, M. (2012) *Benford's Law: Applications for Forensic Accounting, Auditing, and Fraud Detection*. Hoboken, NJ, John Wiley & Sons Inc.

OECD (2004) *OECD Principles of Corporate Governance*. OECD Publishing. Available at: http://dx.doi.org/10.1787/9789264015999-en

Song, W. (2008) 'The Tang Dynasty, a Prosperous Time for Ancient China' *The Epoch Times*, 24 October. Available at www.theepochtimes.com/n2/china-news/tang-taizong-tang-dynasty-ancient-china-6146.html

INDEX

A Commonsense Low Cost Approach to Management (Kaizen), 110–111
Air New Zealand, 109
annual report, 74
AS 8015 (Australian national IT governance standard), 20, 34, 43, 58
ASD-STE100 (ASD-Simplified Technical English standard), 20
ASL, 47
Auditing, 113
Australia, 19–20, 43, 58, 68

B2B/B2C sites, 34
Babbage, Charles, 1–2, 4
Baldrige Foundation Excellence Programme, 75
balloting, 20
Benford's Law, 54
board
   reports, 107, 118
   representatives, 72
Boeing, 20
BS 13500 Standard (UK), 43
budgets, 29
Business Frameworks Study Group, 47
Business Information Service Management Library *see* Business Information Services Library
Business Information Services Library (BiSL), 47
business plans, 1
business representatives, 69–70

Cadbury report 1992, 10
cascading score-card approach, 37, 107, 119, *120*

charter example, 121–123
Charter of Liberties, 73
Chartered Companies Act 1837, 7–8
checklists, xiv
China, 5
CIO, xiv, 107, 112
client relationship management systems (CRM), 71
client representatives, 72
cloud-based solutions, 29, 44, 101
CMMi (Capability Maturity Model Integration), 110
COBIT (Control OBjectives for Information & Related Technology), 58, 109, 113
coding, 95
Companies Acts 1862–1893, 7–8
contracts, 101
corporate risk registers, 104
customers, 34, 50–51, 77–78, 114
Cyrus the Great, 6

Darius I, Emperor, 6–7
data migration, 97
Deloitte's Top 50 fast growing companies, 75
Difference Engine (Babbage), 1, 4
disability, 33

EDM (evaluate direct monitor tasks), 34
employee satisfaction, 115
evaluate-direct-monitor model, 40–41, *41*, 58
eye tests, 33

Farson, Richard, 111
Financial Aspects of Corporate Governance, The see Cadbury report 1992
Form 10-k, 74
Four Pillars of Governance Best Practice, The (IOD), 10–11

Gemba Kaizen (Japanese practice)
   seiketsu (standardise), 52
   seiri (sort out), 51
   seiso (scrub), 51
   seiton (straighten), 51
   shitsuke (sustain), 52
'Governance of Consumer IT in a Business Domain' (SC7 Study Group Report), 46
governance-management value links, 46

Harrison, John, 4
Henry I, King, 73
Herodutus, 6

Icebreaker, 109
implementation
   annual report, 74
   awards, 75
   benefits realisation, 67–68
   board representatives, 72
   business representatives, 69–70
   client representatives, 72
   company profile, 75
   corporate policies, 74–75
   customers, 77–78
   developing a charter, 73
   end users, 76–77

expectations, 73
group questions, *69–70*
introduction, 63–66
inventory, 75–76
IT providers, 77
IT team, 70–72
monitoring agencies/parent companies/subsidiaries, 78
need/gap analysis, 68–69, 72–3
recap, 80–81
shareholder report, 74
stakeholders, 76
statement of intent/equivalent, 74
test strategies, 78–79, 81
training strategies, 80–81
Incas, the, 7
Institute of Directors (Canada), 10
Institute of Directors (Egypt), 10
Institute of Directors (New Zealand), 10
Institute of Directors (UK), 10
investment logic mapping technique (ILM), 68
ISACA framework, 20, 58
ISO 9000 certification, 75
ISO 26000 - Social Responsibility, 11, *12*
ISO 27031: 2011, 75
ISO 31000, 37
ISO standard 38500 (Corporate Governance of ICT)
    business frameworks, 47
    cloud computing, 44
    conformance requirements, 110
    in detail, 21
    digital forensics, 44–45
    direct, 38–40
    evaluation, 35–38
    explanation, xvi, 9–11, 14, 58–59
    fast track process, 19–20
    framework of, 22–34
    guidance, 34, 42, 43–44
    handbooks, 47–48
    implementation of, 15–16, 57, 60–61, 116, *see also* implementation
    interoperability, 45–46
    introduction to, 17–18
    IT audit, 44
    monitoring, 40–42
    part of your compliance framework, 75
    scope of, 21–22
    study group, 18–19
    value of, 18
    voting process, 20
ISO/IEC 15504, 110
ISO/IEC 20000, 77, 110
ISO/IEC 38502 (governance framework diagram), *35*
IT governance
    benefits, 59–60
    business loss, 56
    corporate, 5–11, 13
    cost reduction, 49
    customer satisfaction, 50–51
    description, 2–4, *3*
    financial loss, 54
    handing over, 103
    history, 57–58
    implementation *see* implementation
    increased revenue, 51–52
    management of framework, 99–100
    next steps, 60–61
    optimising frameworks, 109–111
    organisational, 11
    performance improvement, 50
    planning *see* planning
    post-implementation reviews *see* post-implementation reviews
    Principle 1-responsibility, 22, 23–25
    Principle 2-strategy, 23, 25–27
    Principle 3-acquisition, 23, 27–29
    Principle 4-performance, 23, 29–31
    Principle 5-conformance, 23, 31–32, 38
    Principle 6-human behaviour, 23, 32–34, 38
    reputation loss, 55
    responding to market changes, 50
    security breaches, 53
    surprises, 54–55
    sustainable practices, 51
    workplace benefits, 52–53
IT procurement spending, 6
IT security management group, 44
ITIL (international IT service management standard), 4, 47, 77
itSMF framework, 20

John, King, 73

Kaizen, Gemba, 110
Kazaz (example), 122
key goals, 112
key risk indicators (KRIs), 78, 90
KPIs (key performance indicators), 45–46, 64, 79, 88–90, 104, 112

legacy systems, 2

Magna Carta, 73
management
    of framework, 99–102
    reports, 107
    satisfaction, 114
Management of the Absurd (Farson), 111
measuring, 106–107
Microsoft
    PowerPoint, 36
    Windows, 8 33
monitoring, 21, 106–107

need/gap analysis, 68–69, 72–73
New Zealand Treasury Statement of Intent (2012–17), 74
Nigrini, Mark, 54

OECD
    assessment methodology, 9
    guidelines, 8–9, 44
    programme of work, 9
online help systems, 85
operational management
    aligning vendor agreements, 105
    communication, 105–106
    maintaining awareness/acceptance, 104–105
    need for, 102–103
    setting agreements, 104–105
Organisation for Economic Co-operation & Development (OECD), 8–10

PDCA management cycle, 34
Persian Empire, 6–7
Peru, 7
PIR, 102
planning
   deploying governance framework, 96
   developing artefacts, 84–85
   embedding new procedures, 83–84
   going live, 96
   managing/operational workload, 93–94
   modular approach, 83
   problems, 96–7
   process checklists, 92–93
   project prioritisation, 85, *86*, 87, *87*
   reporting lines, 89
   responsibility, 89, 91–92
   reviewing organisational chart, 87–88
   risk, 90
   rolling out framework, 91–92
   signing-off, 97–98, *97*
   supporting systems, 93
   team culture, 89–90
   training/testing, 94–96
post-implementation reviews
   addressing principles to deliver systems, 101–102
   business objectives, 101
   executive summary, 100
   explanation, 100
   introduction, 100–101, 117
   PIR, 102
   preface, 100
   selection /procurement processes, 101

Principles
   1-responsibility, 22, 23–25
   2-strategy, 23, 25–27
   3-acquisition, 23, 27–29
   4-performance, 23, 29–31
   5-conformance, 23, 31–32, 38
   6-human behaviour, 23, 32–34, 38
'process champions', 83
programme management, 102
Public Records Act 2005, 31–32, 92

reporting, 21, 107
risk, 90, 112
   management prioritisation, 46

Sarbanes-Oxley Act 2002 (US), 10, 109
security breaches, 53
self-assessment, 113
service desk teams, 104
shareholders report, 74
stakeholders
   board reports, 118
   feedback from, 113–114
   implementation, 76
   internal, 76
   poor IT governance, 5
   risk, 78, 90
   satisfaction, 115
   security breaches, 53
   training, 80
standards
   BS 13500 (UK), 43
   business continuity planning (ISO 27031), 110
   information security (27000 series), 110

ISO 9000 (certification), 75
ISO 26000 (Social Responsibility), 11, *12*
ISO 27031: 2011, 75
ISO 31000, 37, 110
ISO/IEC 15504, 110
ISO/IEC 20000, 77, 110
ISO/IEC 38502 (governance framework diagram), *35*
steering groups, 105

Tang Taizong, Emperor, 5
teams
   culture, 89–90
   delivery structure, 101
   team building, 87–90
TickIT, 113
time, 29
Tivo, 30
tools, xiii–xiv
Toyota Way, The (Liker), 110–111
training
   ISO/IEC 20000, 24
   ITIL, 24
   modular approach, 83
   new procedures and processes, 83–84
   strategies, 80–81
   and team building, 88
training/testing, 94–96

United Kingdom, 43

wizards, 92–93
work programme planning, *27*
workflow, 92–93
workplace benefits, 52–53

Z Energy, 109